INSPIRATION THREE
for YOU AND YOUR FAMILY

"Who are the great men of the world? . . .
The great man sits next to you, or you
are the person yourself."

—*Acres of Diamonds*

"Trust thyself: every heart vibrates to that
iron string."

—*Self-Reliance*

"Every man is where he is by the law of
his being; the thoughts which he has built
into his character have brought him there."

—*As A Man Thinketh*

INSPIRATION THREE
Three famous classics in one book

Volume I

Acres of Diamonds
Russell Conwell

Essay
on Self-Reliance
Ralph Waldo Emerson

As A Man Thinketh
James Allen

Keats Publishing, Inc. New Canaan, Connecticut

INSPIRATION THREE: Volume I

A Pivot Family Reader

Pivot edition published March, 1973

PIVOT FAMILY READER paperbacks are published by
Keats Publishing, Inc., 212 Elm Street,
New Canaan, Connecticut 06840

CONTENTS

INTRODUCTION

IN A DAY OF mass culture and mass conformity, it is re-
freshing to read the works of Russell Conwell, Ralph
Waldo Emerson and James Allen. In an era when so many
forces crowd in upon the individual, giving us the shape and
taste and inclinations that neither inspire nor challenge,
it is well that we read *Acres of Diamonds* or another
chapter from Emerson. For here were men of vision and
action, writers with dreams that became fulfilled in reality. Our lives need this kind of replenishing, this sense
of nerve and daring, this grasp of greater things that the
world so often stifles and thwarts. They are great teachers,
and blessed will be those who sit at their feet.

Readers will forgive my partiality toward Russell Conwell. His dramatic career has universal appeal and a
special attraction for this writer. As a young lad in New
Jersey, I recall the visits to Baptist Temple in Philadelphia—the great urban church which flourished under
Conwell's leadership—and where my uncle, Dr. Daniel A.
Poling, was to have a distinguished pastorate in the 1930's.

Baptist Temple, and soon thereafter, Temple University,
were the great monuments created by the lecture, "Acres
of Diamonds." Conwell would give all his profits from
this dynamic address to the advancement of good works
and the forwarding of Temple University. It was an amazing record, by an amazing person.

Conwell really lived the lecture he would later give.
raised on a rocky New England farm, he left Yale University to serve in the Civil War. At 19, he was an officer
of his own company, enduring the conflict and remember-

ing forever the sacrifice of Johnny Ring. He began a newspaper, enjoyed a successful law practice, entered the ministry and founded a university. But of all his works and efforts, *Acres of Diamonds* remains as the tower of his achievement.

In this brief essay/lecture you have the secret of his success and perhaps your own; that of finding your resources for success and achievement within your immediate surroundings. In your skills, your household, your neighborhood are the tools for growth and attainment of life goals. Hard to believe? Then read on and reach out for the promises offered by Conwell who gave this lecture more than 5000 times, and now to millions of readers.

Ralph Waldo Emerson adds a fine mixture of practical wisdom to this inspirational collection of famous men; Emerson, the towering individualist. His vision is expressed in his writings, his friendships, his causes. He has the capacity—a century later—to stir the reader to a greater personal effort, a greater understanding of life, and a deeper commitment to high goals and vital relationships. Emerson scolded Presidents when they abused the civil rights of Indians, applauded the abolition of slavery, saluted Thomas Carlyle on a new book and took long walks with Henry Thoreau.

Always, Emerson is pressing for the individual effort, the personal goal, the solitary adventure of the listener. He would not serve the herd nor yield to crowds nor curry favor with the masses. Even so, people thronged after his teaching and lectures. His essay on *Self-Reliance* is a fine introduction to his other works.

Here he writes, "There is a time in every man's education when he arrives at the conviction that envy is ignorance, that imitation is suicide; that he must take himself for better or for worse as his portion; that though the wide universe is full of good, no kernel of nourishing corn can come to him but through his toil bestowed on that plot of ground which is given to him to till."

It is said of Emerson that he "believed in quotation." Indeed, one can almost claim a college education by the writers and scholars that he makes reference to. Yet his own work is eminently quotable: "Society everywhere is in conspiracy against the manhood of every one of its members." Now there is a statement worth pursuing, as soon you will, in this essay. Also, "What I must do is all that concerns me, not what people think." And again, "For nonconformity the world whips you with its displeasure."

James Allen enjoyed literary fame, with acknowledged skill as author and novelist. Yet, of all his works that have been followed for almost a hundred years, *As A Man Thinketh,* is one of the most prized. He certainly did not consider this a major work, but its application has touched thousands and its message is intensely relevant. It follows the theme inherent in the writing of Conwell, that within ourselves is the capacity for success or failure, that our own thoughts and desires will ultimately be fulfilled, and that we have but to cultivate the higher vision, the greater glory for a full and rich life. Allen has an abiding spiritual depth that is comforting and determined, though accompanied by warning and admonition. Life has both, and its journey requires such awareness: "Man is made or unmade by himself; in the armory of thought he forges the weapons by which he destroys himself; he also fashions the tools with which he builds for himself heavenly mansions of joy and strength and peace. By right choice and true application of thought, man ascends to the Divine Perfection; by the abuse and wrong application of thought, he descends below the level of the beast. Between these two extremes are all the grades of character, and man is their maker and master."

Allen is a genius at reaching the currents of our thought processes. Is there not a way to test the following statement by our own experience? He writes:

"To live continually in thoughts of ill will, cynicism, suspicion and envy, is to be confined in a self-made prison. But to think well of all, to find the good in all—such unselfish thoughts are the very portals of heaven. . . ."

Allen does not rule out circumstance, the actions of others for good or ill, yet he determined that our minds be the resource of our strength, not the well of our disbelief and despair.

So we read on and these men will be our guide, prod and instructors. It is fair to say that one cannot be the same after reading and absorbing this wealth of material, aimed at making us self-starters, even self-reliant.

—David Poling

Russell Conwell

ACRES OF
DIAMONDS

ACRES OF DIAMONDS

WHEN GOING DOWN the Tigris and Euphrates rivers many years ago with a party of English travelers I found myself under the direction of an old Arab guide whom we hired up at Bagdad, and I have often thought how that guide resembled our barbers in certain mental characteristics. He thought that it was not only his duty to guide us down those rivers, and do what he was paid for doing, but also to entertain us with stories curious and weird, ancient and modern, strange and familiar. Many of them I have forgotten, and I am glad I have, but there is one I shall never forget.

The old guide was leading my camel by its halter along the banks of those ancient rivers, and he told me story after story until I grew weary of his story-telling and ceased to listen. I have never been irritated with that guide when he lost his temper as I ceased listening. But I remember that he took off his Turkish cap and swung it in a circle to get my attention. I could see it through the corner of my eye, but I determined not to look straight at him for fear he would tell another story. But although I am not a woman, I did finally look, and as soon as I did he went right into another story.

Said he, "I will tell you a story now which I reserve for my particular friends." When he emphasized the words "particular friends," I listened, and I have ever been glad I did. I really feel devoutly thankful that there are 1,674 young men who have been carried through college by this lecture who are also glad that I did listen. The old guide told me that there once lived not far from the River Indus an ancient Persian by the name of Ali Hafed. He said that Ali Hafed owned a very large farm, that he had orchards, grainfields, and gardens; that he had money at interest, and was a wealthy and contented man. He was contented because he was wealthy, and wealthy because he was contented. One day there visited the old Persian farmer one of those ancient Buddhist priests, one of the wise men of the East. He sat down by the fire and told the old farmer how this world of ours was made. He said that this world was once a mere bank of fog, and that the Almighty thrust His finger into this bank of fog, and began slowly to move His finger around, increasing the speed until at last He whirled this bank of fog into a solid ball of fire. Then it went rolling through the universe, burning its way through other banks of fog, and condensed the moisture without, until it fell in floods of rain upon its hot surface, and cooled the outward crust. Then the internal fires bursting outward through the crust threw up the mountains and hills, the valleys, the plains and prairies of this wonderful world of ours. If this internal molten mass came bursting out and cooled very quickly it became granite; less quickly copper, less quickly silver, less quickly gold, and, after gold, diamonds were made.

Said the old priest, "A diamond is a congealed drop of sunlight." Now that is literally scientifically true, that a diamond is an actual deposit of carbon from the sun. The old priest told Ali Hafed that if he had one diamond the size of his thumb he could purchase the county, and if he had a mine of diamonds he could place his children upon thrones through the influence of their great wealth.

Ali Hafed heard all about diamonds, how much they were worth, and went to bed that night a poor man. He had not lost anything, but he was poor because he was discontented, and discontented because he feared he was poor. He said, "I want a mine of diamonds," and he lay awake all night.

Early in the morning he sought out the priest. I know by experience that a priest is very cross when awakened early in the morning, and when he shook that old priest out of his dreams, Ali Hafed said to him:

"Will you tell me where I can find diamonds?"

"Diamonds! What do you want with diamonds?" "Why, I wish to be immensely rich." "Well, then, go along and find them. That is all you have to do; go and find them, and then you have them." "But I don't know where to go."

"Well, if you will find a river that runs through white sands, between high mountains, in those white sands you will always find diamonds." "I don't believe there is any such river." "Oh yes, there are plenty of them. All you have to do is to go and find them, and then you have them." Said Ali Hafed, "I will go."

So he sold his farm, collected his money, left his family in charge of a neighbor, and away he went in search of diamonds. He began his search, very properly to my mind, at the Mountains of the Moon. Afterward he came around into Palestine, then wandered on into Europe, and at last when his money was all spent and he was in rags, wretchedness, and poverty, he stood on the shore of that bay at Barcelona, in Spain, when a great tidal wave came rolling in between the pillars of Hercules, and the poor, afflicted, suffering, dying man could not resist the awful temptation to cast himself into that incoming tide, and he sank beneath its foaming crest, never to rise in this life again.

When that old guide had told me that awfully sad story he stopped the camel I was riding on and went back to fix the baggage that was coming off another camel, and I had an opportunity to muse over his story while he was gone. I remember saying to myself, "Why did he reserve that story for his 'particular friends'?" There seemed to be no beginning, no middle, no end, nothing to it. That was the first story I had ever heard told in my life, and would be the first one I ever read, in which the hero was killed in the chapter. I had but one chapter of that story, and the hero was dead.

When the guide came back and took up the halter of my camel, he went right ahead with the story, into the second chapter, just as though there had been no break. The man who purchased Ali Hafed's farm one day led his camel into the garden to drink, and as that camel put its nose into the shallow water of that garden brook, Ali Hafed's successor noticed a curious flash of light from the white sands of the stream. He pulled out a black stone having an eye of light reflecting all the hues of the rainbow. He took the pebble into the house and put it on the mantel which covers the central fires, and forgot all about it.

A few days later this same old priest came in to visit Ali Hafed's successor, and the moment he opened that drawing-room door he saw that flash of light on the mantel, and he rushed up to it, and shouted: "Here is a diamond! Has Ali Hafed returned?" "Oh no, Ali Hafed has not returned, and that is not a diamond. That is nothing but a stone we found right out here in our own garden." "But," said the priest, "I tell you I know a diamond when I see it. I know positively that is a diamond."

Then together they rushed out into that old garden and stirred up the white sands with their fingers, and lo! there came up other more beautiful and valuable gems than the first. "Thus," said the guide to me, and, friends, it is historically true, "was discovered the diamond mine of Golcanda, the most magnificent diamond mine in all the history of mankind, excelling the Kimberly itself. The Kohinoor, and the Orloff of the crown jewels of England and Russia, the largest on earth, came from that mine."

When that old Arab guide told me the second chapter of his story, he then took off his Turkish cap and swung it around in the air again to get my attention to the moral. Those Arab guides have morals to their stories, although they are not always moral. As he swung his hat, he said to me, "Had Ali Hafed remained at home and dug in his own cellar, or underneath his own wheat fields, or in his own garden, instead of wretchedness, starvation, and death by suicide in a strange land, he would have had 'acres of diamonds.' For every acre of that old farm, yes, every shovelful, afterward revealed gems which since have decorated the crowns of monarchs."

When he had added the moral to his story I saw why he reserved it for "his particular friends." But I did not tell him I could see it. It was that mean old Arab's way of going around a thing like a lawyer, to say indirectly what he did not dare say directly, that "in his private opinion there was a certain young man then traveling down the Tigris River that might better be at home in America." I did not tell him I could see that, but I told him his story reminded me of one, and I told it to him quickly, and I think I will tell it to you.

I told him of a man out in California in 1847, who owned a ranch. He heard they had discovered gold in southern California, and so with a passion for gold he sold his ranch to Colonel Sutter, and away he went, never to come back. Colonel Sutter put a mill upon a stream that ran through that ranch, and one day his little girl brought some wet sand from the raceway into their home and sifted it through her fingers before the fire, and in that falling sand a visitor saw the first shining scales of real gold that were ever discovered in California. The man who had owned that ranch wanted gold, and he could have secured it for the mere taking. Indeed, thirty-eight millions of dollars have been taken out of a very few acres since then. About eight years ago I delivered this lecture in a city that stands on that farm, and they told me that a one-third owner for years and years had been getting one hundred and twenty dollars in gold every fifteen minutes, sleeping or waking, without taxation. You and I would enjoy an income like that—if we didn't have to pay an income tax.

But a better illustration really than that occurred here in our own Pennsylvania. If there is anything I enjoy above another on the platform, it is to get one of these German audiences in Pennsylvania before me, and fire that at them, and I enjoy it tonight. There was a man living in Pennsylvania, not unlike some Pennsylvanians you have seen, who owned a farm, and he did with that farm just what I should do with a farm if I owned one in Pennsylvania—he sold it. But before he sold it he decided to secure

employment collecting coal oil for his cousin,
who was in the business in Canada, where they
first discovered oil on this continent. They
dipped it from the running streams at that early
time. So this Pennsylvania farmer wrote to his
cousin asking for employment. You see, friends,
this farmer was not altogether a foolish man.
No, he was not. He did not leave his farm until
he had something else to do. *Of all the simple-
tons the stars shine on I don't know of a worse
one than the man who leaves one job before
he has gotten another.* That was especial reference to my profession, and has no reference
whatever to a man seeking a divorce. When he
wrote to his cousin for employment, his cousin
replied, "I cannot engage you because you know
nothing about the oil business."

Well, then the old farmer said, "I will know,"
and with most commendable zeal (characteristic
of the students of Temple University) he set
himself at the study of the whole subject. He
began away back at the second day of God's
creation when this world was covered thick and
deep with that rich vegetation which since has
turned to the primitive beds of coal. He studied
the subject until he found that the drainings
really of those rich beds of coal furnished the
coal oil that was worth pumping, and then he
found how it came up with the living springs.
He studied until he knew what it looked like,
smelled like, tasted like, and how to refine it.
Now said he in his letter to his cousin, "I understand the oil business." His cousin answered,
"All right, come on."

So he sold his farm, according to the county record, for $833 (even money, "no cents"). He had scarcely gone from that place before the man who purchased the spot went out to arrange for the watering of the cattle. He found the previous owner had gone out years before and put a plank across the brook back of the barn, edgewise into the surface of the water just a few inches. The purpose of that plank at that sharp angle across the brook was to throw over to the other bank a dreadful-looking scum through which the cattle would not put their noses. But with that plank there to throw it all over to one side, the cattle would drink below, and thus that man who had gone to Canada had been himself damming back for twenty-three years a flood of coal oil which the state geologists of Pennsylvania declared to us ten years later was even then worth a hundred millions of dollars to our state, and four years ago our geologist declared the discovery to be worth to our state a thousand millions of dollars. The man who owned that territory on which the city of Titusville now stands, and those Pleasantville valleys, had studied the subject from the second day of God's creation clear down to the present time. He studied it until he knew all about it, and yet he is said to have sold the whole of it for $833, and again I say, "no sense."

But I need another illustration. I found it in Massachusetts, and I am sorry I did because that is the state I came from. This young man in Massachusetts furnishes just another phase of my thought. He went to Yale College and studied

mines and mining, and became such an adept
as a mining engineer that he was employed by
the authorities of the university to train students
who were behind their classes. During his senior
year he earned $15 a week for doing that work.
When he graduated they raised his pay from
$15 to $45 a week, and offered him a profes-
sorship, and as soon as they did he went right
home to his mother. *If they had raised that boy's
pay from $15 to $15.60 he would have stayed
and been proud of the place, but when they put
it up to $45 at one leap, he said,* "Mother, I won't
work for $45 a week. The idea of a man with
a brain like mine working for $45 a week! Let's
go out in California and stake out gold mines
and silver mines, and be immensely rich."

Said his mother, "Now, Charlie, it is just as
well to be happy as it is to be rich."

"Yes," said Charlie, "but it is just as well to
be rich and happy, too." And they were both
right about it. As he was an only son and she
a widow, of course he had his way. They always do.

They sold out in Massachusetts, and instead
of going to California they went to Wisconsin,
where he went into the employ of the Superior
Copper Mining Company at $15 a week again,
but with the proviso in his contract that he
should have an interest in any mines he should
discover for the company. I don't believe he ever
discovered a mine, and if I am looking in the
face of any stockholder of that copper company,
you wish he had discovered something or other.

I have friends who are not here because they could not afford a ticket, who did have stock in that company at the time this young man was employed there. This young man went out there, and I have not heard a word from him. I don't know what became of him, and I don't know whether he found any mines or not, but I don't believe he ever did.

But I do know the other end of the line. He had scarcely gotten out of the old homestead before the succeeding owner went out to dig potatoes. The potatoes were already growing in the ground when he bought the farm, and as the old farmer was bringing in a basket of potatoes it hugged very tight between the ends of the stone fence. You know in Massachusetts our farms are nearly all stone wall. There you are obliged to be very economical of front gateways in order to have some place to put the stone. When that basket hugged so tight he set it down on the ground, and then dragged on one side, and pulled on the other side, and as he was dragging that basket through this farmer noticed in the upper and outer corner of that stone wall, right next the gate, a block of native silver eight inches square. That professor of mines, mining, and mineralogy, who knew so much about the subject that he would not work for $45 a week, when he sold that homestead in Massachusetts sat right on that silver to make the bargain. He was born on that homestead, was brought up there, and had gone back and forth rubbing the stone with his sleeve until it reflected his countenance, and seemed to say, "Here is a hundred thousand dollars right down here just for the taking." But he would not take it. It was in a home in Newburyport, Massachusetts, and there was no silver there, all away off—well, I don't know where, and he did not, but somewhere else, and he was a professor of mineralogy.

My friends, that mistake is very universally made, and why should we even smile at him. I often wonder what has become of him. I do not know at all, but I will tell you what I "guess" as a Yankee. I guess that he sits out there by his fireside tonight with his friends gathered around him, and he is saying to them something like this: "Do you know that man Conwell who lives in Philadelphia?" "Oh yes, I have heard of him." "Do you know that man Jones who lives in Philadelphia?" "Yes, I have heard of him, too."

Then he begins to laugh, and shakes his sides, and says to his friends, "Well, they have done just the same thing I did, precisely"—and that spoils the whole joke, for you and I have done the same thing he did, and while we sit here and laugh at him he has a better right to sit out there and laugh at us. I know I have made the same mistakes, but, of course, that does not make any difference, because we don't expect the same man to preach and practice, too.

As I come here tonight and look around this audience I am seeing again what through these fifty years I have continually seen—men that are making precisely that same mistake. I often wish

I could see the younger people, and would that the Academy had been filled tonight with our high-school scholars and out grammar-school scholars, that I could have them to talk to. While I would have preferred such an audience as that, because they are most susceptible, as they have not grown up into their prejudices as we have, they have not gotten into any custom that they cannot break, they have not met with any failures as we have; and while I could perhaps do such an audience as that more good than I can do grown-up people, yet I will do the best I can with the material I have. I say to you that you have "acres of diamonds" in Philadelphia right where you now live. "Oh," but you will say, "you cannot know much about your city if you think there are any 'acres of diamonds' here."

I was greatly interested in that account in the newspaper of the young man who found that diamond in North Carolina. It was one of the purest diamonds that has ever been discovered, and it has several predecessors near the same locality. I went to a distinguished professor in mineralogy and asked him where he thought those diamonds came from. The professor secured the map of the geologic formations of our continent, and traced it. He said it went either through the underlying carboniferous strata adapted for such production, westward through Ohio and the Mississippi, or in more probability came eastward through Virginia and up the shore of the Atlantic Ocean. It is a fact that the diamonds were there, for they have been discovered and sold; and that they were carried down there during the drift period, from some northern locality. Now who can say but some person going down with his drill in Philadelphia will find some trace of a diamond mine yet down here? Oh, friends! you cannot say that you are not over one of the greatest diamond mines in the world, for such a diamond as that only comes from the most profitable mines that are found on earth.

But it serves simply to illustrate my thought, which I emphasize by saying if you do not have the actual diamond mines literally you have all that they would be good for to you. Because now that the Queen of England has given the greatest compliment ever conferred upon American woman for her attire because she did not appear with any jewels at all at the late reception in England, it has almost done away with the use of diamonds anyhow. All you would care for would be the few you would wear if you wish to be modest, and the rest you would sell for money.

Now then, I say again that the opportunity to get rich, to attain unto great wealth, is here in Philadelphia now, within the reach of almost every man and woman who hears me speak tonight, and I mean just what I say. I have not come to this platform even under these circumstances to recite something to you. I have come to tell you what in God's sight I believe to be the truth, and if the years of life have been of any value to me in the attainment of common sense, I know I am right; that the men and women sitting here, who found it difficult perhaps to buy a ticket to this lecture or gathering tonight, have within their reach "acres of diamonds," opportunities to get largely wealthy. There never was a place on earth more adapted than the city of Philadelphia today, and never in the history of the world did a poor man without capital have such an opportunity to get rich quickly and honestly as he has now in our city. I say it is the truth, and I want you to accept it as such; for if you think I have come to simply recite something, then I would better not be here. I have no time to waste in any such talk, but to say the things I believe, and unless some of you get richer for what I am saying tonight my time is wasted.

I say that you ought to get rich, and it is your duty to get rich. How many of my pious brethren say to me, "Do you, a Christian minister, spend your time going up and down the country advising young people to get rich, to get money?" "Yes, of course I do." They say, "Isn't that awful! Why don't you preach the gospel instead of preaching about man's making money?" "Because to make money honestly is to preach the gospel." That is the reason. The men who get rich may be the most honest men you find in the community.

"Oh," but says some young man here tonight, "I have been told all my life that if a person has money he is very dishonest and dishonorable and mean and contemptible." My friend, that is the reason why you have none, because you have that idea of people. The foundation of your faith is altogether false. Let me say here clearly, and say it briefly, though subject to discussion which I have not time for here, ninety-eight out of one hundred of the rich men of America are honest. That is why they are rich. That is why they are trusted with money. That is why they carry on great enterprises and find plenty of people to work with them. It is because they are honest men.

Says another young man, "I hear sometimes of men that get millions of dollars dishonestly." Yes, of course you do, and so do I. But they are so rare a thing in fact that the newspapers talk about them all the time as a matter of news until you get the idea that all the other rich men got rich dishonestly.

My friend, you take and drive me—if you furnish the auto—out into the suburbs of Philadelphia, and introduce me to the people who own their homes around this great city, those beautiful homes with gardens and flowers, those magnificent homes so lovely in their art, and I will introduce you to the very best people in character as well as in enterprise in our city, and you know I will. A man is not really a true man until he owns his own home, and they that own their homes are made more honorable and honest and pure, and true and economical and careful, by owning the home.

For a man to have money, even in large sums, is not an inconsistent thing. We preach against covetousness, and you know we do, in the pulpit, and oftentimes preach against it so long and use the terms about "filthy lucre" so extremely that Christians get the idea that when we stand in the pulpit we believe it is wicked for any man to have money—until the collection basket goes around, and then we almost swear at the people because they don't give more money. Oh, the inconsistency of such doctrines as that!

Money is power, and you ought to be reasonably ambitious to have it. You ought because you can do more good with it than you could without it. Money printed your Bible, money builds your churches, money sends your missionaries, and money pays your preachers, and you would not have many of them, either, if you did not pay them. I am always willing that my church should raise my salary, because the church that pays the largest salary always raises it the easiest. You never knew an exception to it in your life. The man who gets the largest salary can do the most good with the power that is furnished to him. Of course he can if his spirit be right to use it for what it is given to him.

I say, then, you ought to have money. If you can honestly attain unto riches in Philadelphia, it is your Christian and godly duty to do so. It is an awful mistake of these pious people to think you must be awfully poor in order to be pious.

Some men say, "Don't you sympathize with the poor people?" Of course I do, or else I would not have been lecturing these years. I won't give in but what I sympathize with the poor, but the number of poor who are to be sympathized with is very small. To sympathize with a man whom God has punished for his sins, thus to help him when God would still continue a just punishment, is to do wrong, no doubt about it, and we do that more than we help those who are deserving. While we should sympathize with God's poor—that is, those who cannot help themselves—let us remember there is not a poor person in the United States who was not made poor by his own shortcomings, or by the shortcomings of someone else. It is all wrong to be poor, anyhow. Let us give in to that argument and pass that to one side.

A gentleman gets up back there, and says, "Don't you think there are some things in this world that are better than money?" Of course I do, but I am talking about money now. Of course there are some things higher than money. Oh yes, I know by the grave that has left me standing alone that there are some things in this world that are higher and sweeter and purer than money. Well do I know there are some things higher and grander than gold. Love is the grandest thing on God's earth, but fortunate the lover who has plenty of money. Money is power, money is force, money will do good as well as harm. In the hands of good men and women it could accomplish, and it has accomplished, good.

I hate to leave that behind me. I heard a man get up in a prayer-meeting in our city and thank the Lord he was "one of God's poor." Well, I wonder what his wife thinks about that? She earns all the money that comes into that house, and he smokes a part of that on the veranda. I don't want to see any more of the Lord's poor of that kind, and I don't believe the Lord does. And yet there are some people who think in order to be pious you must be awfully poor and awfully dirty. That does not follow at all. While we sympathize with the poor, let us not teach a doctrine like that.

Yet the age is prejudiced against advising a Christian man (or, as a Jew would say, a godly man) from attaining unto wealth. The prejudice is so universal and the years are far enough back, I think, for me to safely mention that years ago up at Temple University there was a young man in our theological school who thought he was the only pious student in that department. He came into my office one evening and sat down by my desk, and said to me: "Mr. President, I think it is my duty sir, to come in and labor with you." "What has happened now?" Said he, "I heard you say at the Academy, at the Peirce School commencement, that you thought it was an honorable ambition for a young man to desire to have wealth, and that you thought it made him temperate, made him anxious to have a good name, and made him industrious. You spoke about man's ambition to have money helping to make him a good man. Sir, I have come to tell you the Holy Bible says that 'money is the root of all evil.' "

I told him I had never seen it in the Bible, and advised him to go out into the chapel and get the Bible, and show me the place. So out he went for the Bible, and soon he stalked into my office with the Bible open, with all the bigoted pride of the narrow sectarian, or of one who founds his Christianity on some misinterpretation of Scripture. He flung the Bible down on my desk, and fairly squealed into my ear: "There it is, Mr. President; you can read it for yourself." I said to him: "Well, young man, you will learn when you get a little older that you cannot trust another denomination to read the Bible for you. You belong to another denomination. You are taught in the theological school, however, that emphasis is exegesis. Now, will you take that Bible and read it yourself, and give the proper emphasis to it?"

He took the Bible, and proudly read, " 'The love of money is the root of all evil.' "

Then he had it right, and when one does quote aright from that same old Book he quotes the absolute truth. I have lived through fifty years of the mightiest battle that old Book has ever fought, and I have lived to see its banners flying free; for never in the history of this world did the great minds of earth so universally agree that the Bible is true—all true—as they do at this very hour.

So I say that when he quoted right, of course he quoted the absolute truth. "The love of money is the root of all evil." He who tries to attain unto it too quickly, or dishonestly, will fall into many snares, no doubt about that. The love of money. What is that? It is making an idol of money, and idolatry pure and simple everywhere is condemned by the Holy Scriptures and by man's common sense. The man that worships the dollar instead of thinking of the purposes for which it ought to be used, the man who idolizes simply money, the miser that hordes his money in the cellar, or hides it in his stocking, or refuses to invest it where it will do the world good, that man who hugs the dollar until the eagle squeals has in him the root of all evil.

I think I will leave that behind me now and answer the question of nearly all of you who are asking, "Is there opportunity to get rich in Philadelphia?" Well, now, how simple a thing it is to see where it is, and the instant you see where it is it is yours. Some old gentleman gets up back there and says, "Mr. Conwell, have you lived in Philadelphia for thirty-one years and don't know that the time has gone by when you can make anything in this city?" "No, I don't think it is." "Yes, it is; I have tried it." "What business are you in?" "I kept a store here for twenty years, and never made over a thousand dollars in the whole twenty years."

"Well, then, you can measure the good you have been to this city by what this city has paid you, because a man can judge very well what he is worth by what he receives; that is, in what he is to the world at this time. If you have not made over a thousand dollars in twenty years in Philadelphia, it would have been better for Philadelphia if they had kicked you out of the city nineteen years and nine months ago. A man has no right to keep a store in Philadelphia twenty years and not make at least five hundred thousand dollars, even though it be a corner grocery uptown." You say, "You cannot make five thousand dollars in a store now." Oh, my friends, if you will just take only four blocks around you, and find out what the people want and what you ought to supply and set them down with your pencil, and figure up the profits you would make if you did supply them, you would very soon see it. There is wealth right within the sound of your voice.

Someone says: "You don't know anything about business. A preacher never knows a thing about business." Well, then, I will have to prove that I am an expert. I don't like to do this, but I have to do it because my testimony will not be taken if I am not an expert. My father kept a country store, and if there is any place under the stars where a man gets all sorts of experience in every kind of mercantile transactions, it is in the country store. I am not proud of my experience, but sometimes when my father was away he would leave me in charge of the store, though fortunately for him that was not very often. But this did occur many times, friends: A man would come in the store and say to me, "Do you keep jackknives?" "No, we don't keep jackknives," and I went off whistling a tune. What did I care about that man, anyhow? Then another farmer

would come in and say, "Do you keep jackknives?" "No, we don't keep jackknives." Then
I went away and whistled another tune. Then
a third man came right in the same door and
said, "Do you keep jackknives?" "No. Why is
everyone around here asking for jackknives? Do
you suppose we are keeping this store to supply
the whole neighborhood with jackknives? Do
you carry on your store like that in Philadelphia? The difficulty was I had not then learned
that the foundation of godliness and the foundation principle of success in business are both
the same precisely. The man who says, "I cannot
carry my religion into business" advertises himself either as being an imbecile in business, or
on the road to bankruptcy, or a thief, one of
the three, sure. He will fail within a very few
years. He certainly will if he doesn't carry his
religion into business. If I had been carrying on
my father's store on a Christian plan, godly plan,
I would have had a jackknife for the third man
when he called for it. Then I would have actually done him a kindness, and I would have
received a reward myself, which it would have
been my duty to take.

There are some overpious Christian people
who think if you take any profit on anything
you sell that you are an unrighteous man. On
the contrary, you would be a criminal to sell
goods for less than they cost. You have no right
to do that. You cannot trust a man with your
money who cannot take care of his own. You
cannot trust a man in your family that is not

true to his own wife. You cannot trust a man in the world that does not begin with his own heart, his own character, and his own life. It would have been my duty to have furnished a jackknife to the third man, or the second, and to have sold it to him and actually profited myself. I have no more right to sell goods without making a profit on them than I have to overcharge him dishonestly beyond what they are worth. But I should so sell each bill of goods that the person to whom I sell shall make as much as I make.

To live and let live is the principle of the gospel, and the principle of everyday common sense. Oh, young man, hear me; live as you go along. Do not wait until you have reached my years before you begin to enjoy anything of this life. If I had the millions back, or fifty cents of it, which I have tried to earn in these years, it would not do me anything like the good that it does me now in this almost sacred presence tonight. Oh, yes, I am paid over and over a hundredfold tonight for dividing as I have tried to do in some measure as I went along through the years. I ought not speak that way, it sounds egotistic, but I am old enough now to be excused for that. I should have helped my fellow men, which I have tried to do, and everyone should try to do, and get the happiness of it. The man who goes home with the sense that he has stolen a dollar that day, that he has robbed a man of what was his honest due, is not going to sweet rest. He arises tired in the morning, and goes with an unclean conscience to his work the next day. He is not a successful man at all, although he may have laid up millions. But the man who has gone through life dividing always with his fellow men, making and demanding his own rights and his own profits, and giving to every other man his rights and profits, lives every day, and not only that, but it is the royal road to great wealth. The history of the thousands of millionaires shows that to be the case.

The man over there who said he could not make anything in a store in Philadelphia has been carrying on his store on the wrong principle. Suppose I go into your store tomorrow morning and ask, "Do you know neighbor A, who lives one square away, at house No. 1240?" "Oh yes, I have met him. He deals here at the corner store." "Where did he come from?" "I don't know." "How many does he have in his family?" "I don't know." "What ticket does he vote?" "I don't know." "What church does he go to?" "I don't know, and don't care. What are you asking all these questions for?"

If you had a store in Philadelphia would you answer me like that? If so, then you are conducting your business just as I carried on my father's business in Worthington, Massachusetts. You don't know where your neighbor came from when he moved to Philadelphia, and you don't care. If you had cared you would be a rich man now. If you had cared enough about him to take an interest in his affairs, to find out what he needed, you would have been rich.

But you go through the world saying, "No opportunity to get rich," and there is the fault right at your own door.

But another young man gets up over there and says, "I cannot take up the mercantile business." (While I am talking of trade it applies to every occupation.) "Why can't you go into the mercantile business?" "Because I haven't any capital." Oh, the weak and dudish creature that can't see over its collar! It makes a person weak to see those little dudes standing around the corners and saying, "Oh, if I had plenty of capital, how rich I would get." "Young man, do you think you are going to get rich on capital?" "Certainly." Well, I say, "Certainly not." If your mother has plenty of money, and she will set you up in business, you will "set her up in business," supplying you with capital.

The moment a young man or woman gets more money than he or she has grown to by practical experience, that moment he has gotten a curse. It is no help to a young man or woman to inherit money. It is no help to your children to leave them money, but if you leave them education, if you leave them Christian and noble character, if you leave them a wide circle of friends, if you leave them an honorable name, it is far better than that they should have money. It would be worse for them, worse for the nation, that they should have any money at all. Oh, young man, if you have inherited money, don't regard it as a help. It will curse you through your years, and deprive you of the very best things of human life. There is no class of people to be pitied so much as the inexperienced sons and daughters of the rich of our generation. I pity the rich man's son. He can never know the best things in life.

One of the best things in our life is when a young man has earned his own living, and when he becomes engaged to some lovely young woman, and makes up his mind to have a home of his own. Then with that same love comes also that divine inspiration toward better things, and he begins to save his money. He begins to leave off his bad habits and put money in the bank. When he has a few hundred dollars he goes out in the suburbs to look for a home. He goes to the savings bank, perhaps, for half of the value, and then goes for his wife, and when he takes his bride over the threshold of that door for the first time he says in words of eloquence my voice can never touch: "I have earned this home myself. It is all mine, and I divide with thee." That is the grandest moment a human heart may ever know.

But a rich man's son can never know that. He takes his bride into a finer mansion, it may be, but he is obliged to go all the way through it and say to his wife, "My mother gave me that, my mother gave me that, and my mother gave me this," until his wife wishes she had married his mother. I pity the rich man's son.

The statistics of Massachusetts showed that not one rich man's son out of seventeen ever dies rich. I pity the rich man's sons unless they have the good sense of the elder Vanderbilt, which sometimes happens. He went to his father and said, "Did you earn all your money?" "I did, my son. I began to work on a ferryboat for twenty-five cents a day." "Then," said his son, "I will have none of your money," and he, too, tried to get employment on a ferryboat that Saturday night. He could not get one there, but he did get a place for three dollars a week. Of course, if a rich man's son will do that, he will get the discipline of a poor boy that is worth more than a university education to any man. He would then be able to take care of the millions of his father. But as a rule the rich men will not let their sons do the very thing that made them great. As a rule, the rich man will not allow his son to work—and his mother! Why, she would think it was a social disgrace if her poor, weak, little lily-fingered, sissy sort of a boy had to earn his living with honest toil. I have no pity for such rich men's sons.

I remember one at Niagara Falls. I think I remember one a great deal nearer. I think there are gentlemen present who were at a great banquet, and I beg pardon of his friends. At a banquet here in Philadelphia there sat beside me a kindhearted young man, and he said, "Mr. Conwell, you have been sick for two or three years. When you go out, take my limousine, and it will take you up to your house on Broad Street." I thanked him very much, and perhaps I ought not to mention the incident in this way, but I follow the facts. I got onto the seat with the driver of that limousine, outside, and when we were going up I asked the driver, "How much did this limousine cost?" "Six thousand eight hundred, and he had to pay the duty on it." "Well," I said, "does the owner of this machine ever drive it himself?" At that the chauffeur laughed so heartily that he lost control of his machine. He was so surprised at that question that he ran up on the sidewalk, and around a corner lamp post out into the street again. And when he got out into the street he laughed till the whole machine trembled. He said: "He drive this machine! Oh, he would be lucky if he knew enough to get out when we get there."

I must tell you about a rich man's son at Niagara Falls. I came in from the lecture to the hotel, and as I approached the desk of the clerk there stood a millionaire's son from New York. He was an indescribable specimen of anthropologic impotency. He had a skullcap on one side of his head, with a gold tassel in the top of it, and a gold-headed cane under his arm with more in it than in his head. It is a difficult thing to describe that young man. He wore an eyeglass that he could not see through, patent-leather boots that he could not walk in, and pants that he could not sit down in—dressed like a grasshopper. This human cricket came up to the clerk's desk just as I entered, adjusted his unseeing eyeglass, and spake in this wise to the clerk. You see, he thought it was "Hinglish, you know," to lisp. "Thir, will you have the kindneth to thupply me with thome papah and enwelophs!" The hotel clerk measured that man quick, and he pulled the envelopes and paper out of a drawer, threw them across the counter toward the young man, and then turned away to his books. You should have seen that young man when those envelopes came across that counter. He swelled up like a gobbler turkey, adjusted his unseeing eyeglass, and yelled: "Come right back here. Now thir, will you order a thervant to take that papah and enwelophs to yondah dethk." Oh, the poor, miserable, contemptible American monkey! He could not carry paper and envelopes twenty feet. I suppose he could not get his arms down to do it. I have no pity for such travesties upon human nature. If you have not capital, young man, I am glad of it. What you need is common sense, not copper cents.

The best thing I can do is to illustrate by actual facts well-known to you all. A. T. Stewart, a poor boy in New York, had $1.50 to begin life on. He lost 87½ cents of that on the very first venture. How fortunate that young man who loses the first time he gambles. That boy said, "I will never gamble again in business," and he never did. How came he to lose 87½ cents? You probably all know the story how he lost it— because he bought some needles, threads, and buttons to sell which people did not want, and had them left on his hands, a dead loss. Said the boy, "I will not lose any more money in that way." Then he went around first to the doors and asked the people what they did want.

Then when he had found out what they wanted he invested his 62½ cents to supply a known demand. Study it wherever you choose—in business, in your profession, in your housekeeping, whatever your life, that one thing is the secret of success. You must first know the demand. You must first know what people need, and then invest yourself where you are most needed. A. T. Stewart went on that principle until he was worth what amounted afterward to forty millions of dollars, owning the very store in which Mr. Wanamaker carries on his great work in New York. His fortune was made by losing something, which taught him the great lesson that he must only invest himself or his money in something that people need. When will you salesmen learn it? When will you manufacturers learn that you must know the changing needs of humanity if you would succeed in life? Apply yourselves, all you Christian people, as manufacturers or merchants or workmen to supply that human need. It is a great principle as broad as humanity and as deep as the Scripture itself.

The best illustration I ever heard was of John Jacob Astor. You know that he made the money of the Astor family when he lived in New York. He came across the sea in debt for his fare. But that poor boy with nothing in his pocket made the fortune of the Astor family on one principle. Some young man here tonight will say, "Well, they could make those fortunes over in New York, but they could not do it in Philadelphia!" My friends, did you ever read that wonderful book of Riis (his memory is sweet to us because of his recent death), wherein is given his statistical account of the records taken in 1889 of 107 millionaires of New York? If you read the account you will see that out of the 107 millionaires only seven made their money in New York. Out of the 107 millionaires worth ten million dollars in real estate then, 67 of them made their money in towns of less than 3,500 inhabitants. The richest man in this country today, if you read the real estate values, has never moved away from a town of 3,500 inhabitants. It makes not so much difference where you are as who you are. But if you cannot get rich in Philadelphia you certainly cannot do it in New York.

Now John Jacob Astor illustrated what can be done anywhere. He had a mortgage once on a millinery store, and they could not sell bonnets enough to pay the interest on his money. So he foreclosed that mortgage, took possession of the store, and went into partnership with the very same people, in the same store, with the same capital. He did not give them a dollar of capital. They had to seel goods to get any money. Then he left them alone in the store just as they had been before, and he went out and sat down on a bench in the park in the shade. What was John Jacob Astor doing out there, and in partnership with people who had failed on his own hands? He had the most important and, to my mind, the most pleasant part of that partnership on his hands. For as John Jacob Astor sat on that bench he was watching the ladies as they went by; and where is the man who would not get rich at that business? As he sat on the bench if a lady passed him with her shoulders back and head up, and looked straight to the front, as if she did not care if all the world did gaze on her, then he studied her bonnet, and by the time it was out of sight he knew the shape of the frame, the color of the trimmings, and the crinklings in the feather. I sometimes try to describe a bonnet, but not always. I would not try to describe a modern bonnet. Where is the man that could describe one? This aggregation of all sorts of driftwood stuck on the back of the head, or the side of the neck, like a rooster with only one tail feather left. But in John Jacob Astor's day there was some art about the millinery business, and he went to the millinery store and said to them: "Now put into the show window just such a bonnet as I describe to you, because I have already seen a lady who likes such a bonnet. Don't make up any more until I come back." The he went out and sat down again, and another lady passed him of a different form, of different complexion, with a different shape and color of bonnet. "Now," said he, "put such a bonnet as that in the show window." He did not fill his show window uptown with a lot of hats and bonnets to drive people away, and then sit on the back stairs and bawl because people went to Wanamaker's to trade. He did not have a hat or a bonnet in that show window but what some lady liked before it was made up. The tide of

custom began immediately to turn in, and that
has been the foundation of the greatest store
in New York in that line, and still exists as one
of three stores. Its fortune was made by John
Jacob Astor after they had failed in business,
not by giving them any more money, but by
finding out what the ladies liked for bonnets
before they wasted any material in making them
up. I tell you if a man could foresee the millinery
business he could foresee anything under
heaven!

Suppose I were to go through this audience
tonight and ask you in this great manufacturing
city if there are not opportunities to get rich in
manufacturing. "Oh yes," some young man says,
"there are opportunities here still if you build
with some trust and if you have two or three
millions of dollars to begin with as capital."
Young man, the history of the breaking up of
the trusts by that attack upon "big business"
is only illustrating what is now the opportunity
of the smaller man. The time never came in the
history of the world when you could get rich
so quickly manufacturing without capital as you
can now.

But you will say, "You cannot do anything
of the kind. You cannot start without capital."
Young man, let me illustrate for a moment. I
must do it. It is my duty to every young man
and woman, because we are all going into business very soon on the same plan. Young man,
remember if you know what people need you
have gotten more knowledge of a fortune than
any amount of capital can give you.

There was a poor man out of work living in Hingham, Massachusetts. He lounged around the house until one day his wife told him to get out and work, and, as he lived in Massachusetts, he obeyed his wife. He went out and sat down on the shore of the bay, and whittled a soaked shingle into a wooden chain. His children that evening quarreled over it, and he whittled a second one to keep peace. While he was whittling the second one a neighbor came in and said: "Why don't you whittle toys and sell them? You could make money at that." "Oh," he said, "I would not know what to make." "Why don't you ask your own children right here in your own house what to make?" "What is the use of trying that?" said the carpenter. "My children are different from other people's children." (I used to see people like that when I taught school.) But he acted upon the hint, and the next morning when Mary came down the stairway, he asked, "What do you want for a toy?" She began to tell him she would like a doll's bed, a doll's washstand, a doll's carriage, a little doll's umbrella, and went on with a list of things that would take him a lifetime to supply. So, consulting his own children, in his own house, he took the firewood, for he had no money to buy lumber, and whittled those strong, unpainted Hingham toys that were for so many years known all over the world. That man began to make those toys for his own children, and then made copies and sold them through the boot-and-shoe store next door. He began to make a little money, and then a little more, and Mr. Lawson, in his *Frenzied Finance* says that man is the richest man in old Massachusetts, and I think it is the truth. And that man is worth a hundred millions of dollars today, and has been only thirty-four years making it on that one principle—that one must judge that what his own children like at home other people's children would like in their homes, too; to judge the human heart by oneself, by one's wife or by one's children is the royal road to success in manufacturing. "Oh," but you say, "didn't he have any capital?" Yes, a penknife, but I don't know that he had paid for that.

I spoke thus to an audience in New Britain, Connecticut, and a lady four seats back went home and tried to take off her collar, and the collar button stuck in the buttonhole. She threw it out and said, "I am going to get up something better than that to put on collars." Her husband said: "After what Conwell said tonight, you see there is a need of an improved collar fastener that is easier to handle. There is a human need; there is a great fortune. Now, then, get up a collar button and get rich." He made fun of her, and consequently made fun of me, and that is one of the saddest things which comes over me like a deep cloud of midnight sometimes— although I have worked so hard for more than half a century, yet how little I have ever really done. Notwithstanding the greatness and the handsomeness of your compliment tonight, I do not believe there is one in ten of you that is going to make a million of dollars because you are here tonight; but it is not my fault, it is yours. I say that sincerely. What is the use of my talking if people never do what I advise them to do? When her husband ridiculed her, she made up her mind she would make a better collar button, and when a woman makes up her mind "she will," and does not say anything about it, she does it. It was that New England woman who invented the snap button which you can find anywhere now. It was first a collar button with a spring cap attached to the outer side. Any of you who wear modern waterproofs know the button that simply pushes together, and when you unbutton it you simply pull it apart. That is the button to which I refer, and which she invented. She afterward invented several other buttons, and then invested in more, and then was taken into partnership with great factories. Now that woman goes over the sea every summer in her private steamship—yes, and takes her husband with her! If her husband were to die, she would have money enough left now to buy a foreign duke or count or some such title as that at the latest quotations.

Now what is my lesson in that incident? It is this: I told her then, though I did not know her, what I now say to you, "Your wealth is too near to you. You are looking right over it"; and she had to look over it because it was right under her chin.

I have read in the newspaper that a woman never invented anything. Well, that newspaper ought to begin again. Of course, I do not refer to gossip—I refer to machines—and if I did I might better include the men. That newspaper could never appear if women had not invented something. Friends, think. Ye women, think! You say you cannot make a fortune because you are in some laundry, or running a sewing machine, it may be, or walking before some loom, and yet you can be a millionaire if you will but follow this almost infallible direction.

When you say a woman doesn't invent anything, I ask, Who invented the Jacquard loom that wove every stitch you wear? Mrs. Jacquard. The printer's roller, the printing press, were invented by farmers' wives. Who invented the cotton gin of the South that enriched our country so amazingly? Mrs. General Greene invented the cotton gin and showed the idea to Mr. Whitney, and he, like a man, seized it. Who was it that invented the sewing machine? If I would go to school tomorrow and ask your children they would say, "Elias Howe."

He was in the Civil War with me, and often in my tent, and I often heard him say that he worked fourteen years to get up that sewing machine. But his wife made up her mind one day that they would starve to death if there wasn't something or other invented pretty soon, and so in two hours she invented the sewing machine. Of course he took out the patent in his name. Men always do that. Who was it that invented the mower and the reaper? According to Mr. McCormick's confidential communication, so recently published, it was a West

Virginia woman, who, after his father and he had failed altogether in making a reaper and gave it up, took a lot of shears and nailed them together on the edge of a board, with one shaft of each pair loose, and then wired them so that when she pulled the wire one way it closed them, and when she pulled the wire the other way it opened them, and there she had the principle of the mowing machine. If you look at a mowing machine, you will see it is nothing but a lot of shears. If a woman can invent a mowing machine, if a woman can invent a Jacquard loom, if a woman can invent a cotton gin, if a woman can invent a trolley switch—as she did and made the trolleys possible; if a woman can invent, as Mrs. Carnegie said, the great iron squeezers that laid the foundation of all the steel millions of the United States, "we men" can invent anything under the stars! I say that for the encouragement of the men.

Who are the great inventors of the world? Again this lesson comes before us. The great inventor sits next to you, or you are the person yourself. "Oh," but you will say, "I have never invented anything in my life." Neither did the great inventors until they discovered one great secret. Do you think it is a man with a head like a bushel measure or a man like a stroke of lightning? It is neither. The really great man is a plain, straightforward, everyday, common-sense man. You would not dream that he was a great inventor if you did not see something he had actually done. His neighbors do not re-

gard him as so great. You never see anything
great over your back fence. You say there is no
greatness among your neighbors. It is all away
off somewhere else. Their greatness is ever so
simple, so plain, so earnest, so practical, that
the neighbors and friends never recognize it.

True greatness is often unrecognized. That is
sure. You do not know anything about the greatest men and women. I went out to write the
life of General Garfield, and a neighbor, knowing I was in a hurry, and as there was a great
crowd around the front door, took me around
to General Garfield's back door and shouted,
"Jim! Jim!" And very soon "Jim" came to the
door and let me in, and I wrote the biography
of one of the grandest men of the nation, and
yet he was just the same old "Jim" to his neighbor. If you know a great man in Philadelphia
and you should meet him tomorrow, you would
say, "How are you, Sam?" or "Good morning,
Jim." Of course you would. That is just what
you would do.

One of my soldiers in the Civil War had been
sentenced to death, and I went up to the White
House in Washington—went there for the first
time in my life—to see the President. I went into
the waiting room and sat down with a lot of
others on the benches, and the secretary asked
one after another to tell him what they wanted.
After the secretary had been through the line,
he went in, and then came back to the door and
motioned for me. I went up to that anteroom,
and the secretary said: "That is the President's

door right over there. Just rap on it and go right in." I never was so taken aback, friends, in all my life, never. The secretary himself made it worse for me, because he had told me how to go in and then went out another door to the left and shut that. There I was, in the hallway by myself before the President of the United States of America's door. I had been on fields of battle, where the shells did sometimes shriek and the bullets did sometimes hit me, but I always wanted to run. I have no sympathy with the old man who says, "I would just as soon march up to the cannon's mouth as eat my dinner." I have no faith in a man who doesn't know enough to be afraid when he is being shot at. I never was so afraid when the shells came around us at Antietam as I was when I went into that room that day; but I finally mustered the courage—I don't know how I ever did—and at arm's length tapped on the door. The man inside did not help me at all, but yelled out, "Come in and sit down!"

Well, I went in and sat down on the edge of a chair, and wished I were in Europe, and the man at the table did not look up. He was one of the world's greatest men, and was made great by one single rule. Oh, that all the young people of Philadelphia were before me now and I could say just this one thing, and that they would remember it. I would give a lifetime for the effect it would have on our city and on civilization. Abraham Lincoln's principle for greatness can be adopted by nearly all. This was his rule:

Whatsoever he had to do at all, he put his whole mind into it and held it all there until that was all done. That makes men great almost anywhere. He stuck to those papers at that table and did not look up at me, and I sat there trembling. Finally, when he had put the string around his papers, he pushed them over to one side and looked over to me, and a smile came over his worn face. He said: "I am a very busy man and have only a few minutes to spare. Now tell me in the fewest words what it is you want." I began to tell him, and mentioned the case, and he said: "I have heard all about it and you do not need to say any more. Mr. Stanton was talking to me only a few days ago about that. You can go to the hotel and rest assured that the President never did sign an order to shoot a boy under twenty years of age, and never will. You can say that to his mother anyhow."

Then he said to me, "How is it going in the field?" I said, "We sometimes get discouraged." And he said: "It is all right. We are going to win out now. We are getting very near the light. No man ought to wish to be President of the United States, and I will be glad when I get through; then Tad and I are going out to Springfield, Illinois. I have bought a farm out there and I don't care if I again earn only twenty-five cents a day. Tad has a mule team, and we are going to plant onions."

Then he asked me, "Were you brought up on a farm?" I said, "Yes; in the Berkshire Hills of Massachusetts." He then threw his leg over the corner of the big chair and said, "I have heard many a time, ever since I was young, that up there in those hills you have to sharpen the noses of the sheep in order to get down to the grass between the rocks." He was so familiar, so everyday, so farmer-like, that I felt right at home with him at once.

He then took hold of another roll of paper, and looked up at me and said, "Good morning." I took the hint then and got up and went out. After I had gotten out I could not realize I had seen the President of the United States at all. But a few days later, when still in the city, I saw the crowd pass through the East Room by the coffin of Abraham Lincoln, and when I looked at the upturned face of the murdered President I felt then that the man I had seen such a short time before, who, so simple a man, so plain a man, was one of the greatest men that God ever raised up to lead a nation on to ultimate liberty. Yet he was only "Old Abe" to his neighbors. When they had the second funeral, I was invited among others, and went out to see that same coffin put back in the tomb at Springfield. Around the tomb stood Lincoln's old neighbors, to whom he was just "Old Abe." Of course that is all they would say.

Did you ever see a man who struts around altogether too large to notice an ordinary working mechanic? Do you think he is great? He is nothing but a puffed-up balloon, held down by his big feet. There is no greatness there.

Who are the great men and women? My attention was called the other day to the history of a very little thing that made the fortune of a very poor man. It was an awful thing, and yet because of that experience he—not a great inventor or genius—invented the pin that now is called the safety pin, and out of that safety pin made the fortune of one of the great aristocratic families of this nation.

A poor man in Massachusetts who had worked in the nail-works was injured at thirty-eight, and he could earn but little money. He was employed in the office to rub out the marks on the bills made by pencil memorandums, and he used a rubber until his hand grew tired. He then tied a piece of rubber on the end of a stick and worked it like a plane. His little girl came and said, "Why, you have a patent, haven't you?" The father said afterward, "My daughter told me when I took that stick and put the rubber on the end that there was a patent, and that was the first thought of that." He went to Boston and applied for his patent, and every one of you that has a rubber-tipped pencil in your pocket is now paying tribute to the millionaire. No capital, not a penny did he invest in it. All was income, all the way up into the millions.

But let me hasten to one other greater thought. "Show me the great men and women who live in Philadelphia." A gentleman over there will get up and say: "We don't have any great men in Philadelphia. They don't live here. They live away off in Rome or St. Petersburg or London or Manayunk, or anywhere else but here in our town." I have come now to the apex of my thought. I have come now to the heart of the whole matter and to the center of my struggle: Why isn't Philadelphia a greater city in its greater wealth? Why does New York excel Philadelphia? People say, "Because of her harbor." Why do many other cities of the United States get ahead of Philadelphia now? There is only one answer, and that is because our own people talk down their own city. If there ever was a community on earth that has to be forced ahead, it is the city of Philadelphia. If we are to have a boulevard, talk it down; if we are going to have better schools, talk them down; if you wish to have wise legislation, talk it down; talk all the proposed improvements down. That is the only great wrong that I can lay at the feet of the magnificent Philadelphia that has been so universally kind to me. I say it is time we turn around in our city and begin to talk up the things that are in our city, and begin to set them before the world as the people of Chicago, New York, St. Louis, and San Francisco do. Oh, if we only could get that spirit out among our people, that we can do things in Philadelphia and do them well!

Arise, ye millions of Philadelphians, trust in God and man, and believe in the great opportunities that are right here—not over in New York or Boston, but here—for business, for everything that is worth living for on earth. There was never an opportunity greater. Let us talk up our own city.

But there are two other young men here tonight, and that is all I will venture to say, because it is too late. One over there gets up and says, "There is going to be a great man in Philadelphia, but never was one." "Oh, is that so? When are you going to be great?" "When I am elected to some political office." Young man, won't you learn a lesson in the primer of politics that it is a *prima facie* evidence of littleness to hold office under our form of government? Great men get into office sometimes, but what this country needs is men that will do what we tell them to do. This nation—where the people rule—is governed by the people, for the people, and so long as it is, then the officeholder is but the servant of the people, and the Bible says the servant cannot be greater than the master. The Bible says, "He that is sent cannot be greater than He who sent him." The people rule, or should rule, and if they do, we do not need the greater men in office. If the great men in America took our offices, we would change to an empire in the next ten years.

I know of a great many young women, now that woman's suffrage is coming, who say, "I am going to be President of the United States some day." I believe in woman's suffrage, and there is no doubt but what it is coming, and I am getting out of the way, anyhow. I may want an office by and by myself; but if the ambition for an office influences the women in their desire to vote, I want to say right here what I say to the young men, that if you only get the privilege of casting one vote, you don't get anything that is worth while. Unless you can control more than one vote, you will be unknown, and your influence so dissipated as practically not to be felt. This country is not run by votes. Do you think it is? It is governed by influence. It is governed by the ambitions and the enterprises which control votes. The young woman who thinks she is going to vote for the sake of holding an office is making an awful blunder.

That other young man gets up and says, "There are going to be great men in this country and in Philadelphia." "Is that so? When?" "When there comes a great war, when we get into difficulty through watchful waiting in Mexico; when we get into war with England over some frivolous deed, or with Japan or China or New Jersey or some distant country. Then I will march up to the cannon's mouth; I will sweep up among the glistening bayonets; I will leap into the arena and tear down the flag and bear it away in triumph. I will come home with stars on my shoulder, and hold every office in the gift of the nation, and I will be great." No, you won't. You think you are going to be made great by an office, but remember that if you are not great before you get the office, you won't be great when you secure it. It will only be a burlesque in that shape.

We had a Peace Jubilee here after the Spanish War. Out West they don't believe this, because they said, "Philadelphia would not have heard of any Spanish War until fifty years hence."

Some of you saw the procession go up Broad Street. I was away, but the family wrote to me that the tally-ho coach with Lieutenant Hobson upon it stopped right at the front door and the people shouted, "Hurrah for Hobson!" and if I had been there I would have yelled too, because he deserves much more of his country than he has ever received. But suppose I go into school and say, "Who sank the *Merrimac* at Santiago?" and if the boys answer me, "Hobson," they will tell me seven-eighths of a lie. There were seven other heroes on that steamer, and they, by virtue of their position, were continually exposed to the Spanish fire, while Hobson, as an officer, might reasonably be behind the smokestack. You have gathered in this house your most intelligent people, and yet, perhaps, not one here can name the other seven men.

We ought not to so teach history. We ought to teach that, however humble a man's station may be, if he does his full duty in that place he is just as much entitled to the American people's honor as is the king upon his throne. But we do not so teach. We are now teaching everywhere that the generals do all the fighting.

I remember that, after the war, I went down to see General Robert E. Lee, that magnificent Christian gentleman of whom both North and South are now proud as one of our great Americans. The general told me about his servant, Rastus, who was an enlisted colored soldier. He called him in one day to make fun of him, and said, "Rastus, I hear that all the rest of your company are killed, and why are you not killed?" Rastus winked at him and said, " 'Cause when there is any fightin' goin' on I stay back with the generals."

I remember another illustration. I would leave it out but for the fact that when you go to the library to read this lecture, you will find this has been printed in it for twenty-five years. I shut my eyes—shut them close—and lo! I see the faces of my youth. Yes, they sometimes say to me, "Your hair is not white; you are working night and day without seeming ever to stop; you can't be old." But when I shut my eyes, like any other man of my years, oh, then come trooping back the faces of the loved and lost of long ago, and I know, whatever men may say, it is evening time.

I shut my eyes now and look back to my native town in Massachusetts, and I see the cattle-show ground on the mountaintop; I can see the horse sheds there. I can see the Congregational Church; see the town hall and mountaineers' cottages; see a great assembly of people turning out, dressed resplendently, and I can see flags flying and handkerchiefs waving and hear bands playing. I can see that company of soldiers that had re-enlisted marching up on that cattle-show ground. I was but a boy, but I was captain of that company and puffed out with pride. A cambric needle would have burst me all to pieces. Then I thought it was the greatest event

that ever came to man on earth. If you have
ever thought you would like to be a king or
queen, you go and be received by the mayor.

The bands played, and all the people turned
out to receive us. I marched up that Common
so proud at the head of my troops, and we
turned down into the town hall. Then they
seated my soldiers down the center aisle and
I sat down on the front seat. A great assembly
of people—a hundred or two—came in to fill the
town hall, so that they stood up all around. Then
the town officers came in and formed a half
circle. The mayor of the town sat in the middle
of the platform. He was a man who had never
held office before; but he was a good man, and
his friends have told me that I might use this
without giving them offense. He was a good
man, but he thought an office made a man great.
He came up and took his seat, adjusted his powerful spectacles, and looked around, when he
suddenly spied me sitting there on the front seat.
He came right forward on the platform and
invited me up to sit with the town officers. No
town officer ever took any notice of me before
I went to war, except to advise the teacher to
thrash me, and now I was invited up on the
stand with the town officers. Oh my! the town
mayor was then the emperor, the king of our
day and our time. As I came up on the platform
they gave me a chair about this far, I would
say, from the front.

When I had got seated, the chairman of the
Selectmen arose and came forward to the table,

and we all supposed he would introduce the
Congregational minister, who was the only orator in town, and that he would give the oration
to the returning soldiers. But, friends, you
should have seen the surprise which ran over
the audience when they discovered that the old
fellow was going to deliver that speech himself.
He had never made a speech in his life, but he
fell into the same error that hundreds of other
men have fallen into. It seems so strange that
a man won't learn he must speak his piece as
a boy if he intends to be an orator when he
is grown, but he seems to think all he has to
do is to hold an office to be a great orator.

So he came up to the front, and brought with
him a speech which he had learned by heart
walking up and down the pasture, where he had
frightened the cattle. He brought the manuscript
with him and spread it out on the table so as
to be sure he might see it. He adjusted his spectacles and leaned over it for a moment and
marched back on that platform, and then came
forward like this—tramp, tramp, tramp. He must
have studied the subject a great deal, when you
come to think of it, because he assumed an
"elocutionary" attitude. He rested heavily upon
his left heel, threw back his shoulders, slightly
advanced the right foot, opened the organs of
speech, and advanced his right foot at an angle
of forty-five. As he stood in that elocutionary
attitude, friends, this is just the way that speech
went. Some people say to me, "Don't you exag-
gerate?" That would be impossible. But I am

here for the lesson and not for the story, and
this is the way it went:

"Fellow citizens—" As soon as he heard his
voice his fingers began to go like that, his knees
began to shake, and then he trembled all over.
He choked and swallowed and came around to
the table to look at the manuscript. Then he
gathered himself up with clenched fists and
came back: "Fellow citizens, we are—Fellow
citizens, we are—we are—we are—we are—we
are—we are very happy—we are very happy—we
are very happy. We are very happy to welcome
back to their native town these soldiers who
have fought and bled—and come back again to
their native town. We are especially—we are
especially—we are especially. We are especially
pleased to see with us today this young hero"
(that meant me)—"this young hero who in imagination" (friends, remember he said that; if he
had not said "in imagination" I would not be
egotistic enough to refer to it at all)—"this young
hero who in imagination we have seen leading—we have seen leading—leading. We have
seen leading his troops on to the deadly breach.
We have seen his shining—we have seen his
shining—his shining—his shining sword—flashing. Flashing in the sunlight, as he shouted to
his troops, 'Come on'!"

Oh dear, dear, dear! how little that good man
knew about war. If he had known anything
about war at all he ought to have known what
any of my G. A. R. comrades here tonight will
tell you is true, that it is next to a crime for

an officer of infantry ever in time of danger to
go ahead of his men. "He, with his shining sword
flashing in the sunlight, shouting to his troops,
'Come on'!" I never did it. Do you suppose I
would get in front of my men to be shot in front
by the enemy and in the back by my own men?
That is no place for an officer. The place for the
officer in actual battle is behind the line. How
often, as a staff officer, I rode down the line,
when our men were suddenly called to the line
of battle, and the Rebel yells were coming out
of the woods, and shouted: "Officers to the rear!
Officers to the rear!" Then every officer gets
behind the line of private soldiers, and the
higher the officer's rank the farther behind he
goes. Not because he is any the less brave, but
because the laws of war require that. And yet
he shouted, "He, with his shining sword—" In
that house there sat the company of my soldiers
who had carried that boy across the Carolina
rivers that he might not wet his feet. Some of
them had gone far out to get a pig or a chicken.
Some of them had gone to death under the
shell-swept pines in the mountains of Tennes-
see, yet in the good man's speech they were
scarcely known. He did refer to them, but only
incidentally. The hero of the hour was this boy.
Did the nation owe him anything? No, nothing
then and nothing now. Why was he the hero?
Simply because that man fell into that same
human error—that this boy was great because
he was an officer and these were only private
soldiers.

Oh, I learned the lesson then that I will never forget so long as the tongue of the bell of time continues to swing for me. Greatness consists not in the holding of some future office, but really consists in doing great deeds with little means and the accomplishment of vast purposes from the private ranks of life. To be great at all one must be great here, now, in Philadelphia. He who can give to this city better streets and better sidewalks, better schools and more colleges, more happiness and more civilization, more of God, he will be great anywhere. Let every man or woman here, if you never hear me again, remember this, that if you wish to be great at all, you must begin where you are and with what you are, in Philadelphia, now. He who can give to his city any blessing, he who can be a good citizen while he lives here, he who can make better homes, he who can be a blessing whether he works in the shop or sits behind the counter or keeps house, whatever be his life, he who would be great anywhere must first be great in his own Philadelphia.

Ralph Waldo Emerson

~ ~

ESSAY ON
SELF-RELIANCE

SELF-RELIANCE

MAN IS his own star; and the soul that can
Render an honest and a perfect man,
Commands all light, all influence, all fate;
Nothing to him falls early or too late.
Our acts our angels are, or good or ill,
Our fatal shadows that walk by us still.

From the
EPILOGUE TO HONEST MAN'S FORTUNE
(Beaumont and Fletcher)

SELF-RELIANCE

I READ THE other day some verses written by an eminent painter which were original and not conventional. The soul always hears an admonition in such lines, let the subject be what it may. The sentiment they instil is of more value than any thought they may contain. To believe your own thought, to believe that what is true for you in your private heart is true for all men,—that is genius. Speak your latent conviction, and it shall be the universal sense; for the inmost in due times becomes the outmost, and our first thought is rendered back to us by the trumpets of the Last Judgment. Familiar as the voice of the mind is to each, the highest merit we ascribe to Moses, Plato and Milton is that they set at naught books and traditions, and spoke not what men, but what *they* thought. A man should learn to detect and watch that gleam of light which flashes across his mind from within, more than the lustre of the firmament of bards and sages. Yet he dismisses without notice his thought, because it is his. In every work of genius we recognize our own rejected thoughts; they come back to us with a certain alienated majesty. Great works of art have no more affecting lesson for us than this. They teach us to abide by our spontaneous impression with good-humored inflexibility then most when the whole cry of voices is on the other side. Else to-morrow a stranger will say with masterly good sense precisely what we have thought and felt all the time, and we shall be forced to take with shame our own opinion from another.

There is a time in every man's education when he arrives at the conviction that envy is ignorance; that imitation is suicide; that he must take himself for better for worse as his portion; that though the wide universe is full of good, no kernel of nourishing corn can come to him but through his toil bestowed on that plot of ground which is given to him to till. The power which resides in him is new in nature, and none but he knows what that is which he can do, nor does he know until he has tried. Not for nothing one face, one character, one fact, makes much impression on him, and another none. This sculpture in the memory is not without pre-established harmony. The eye was placed where one ray should fall, that it might testify of that particular ray. We but half express ourselves, and are ashamed of that divine idea which each of us represents. It may be safely trusted as proportionate and of good issues, so it be faithfully imparted, but God will not have his work made manifest by cowards. A man is relieved and gay when he has put his heart into his work and done his best; but what he has said or done otherwise shall give him no peace. It is a deliverance which does not deliver. In the attempt his genius deserts him; no muse befriends; no invention, no hope.

Trust thyself: every heart vibrates to that iron string. Accept the place the divine providence has found for you, the society of your contemporaries, the connection of events. Great men have always done so, and confided themselves childlike to the genius of their age, betraying their perception that the absolutely trustworthy was seated at their heart, working through their hands, predominating in all their being. And we are now men, and must accept in the highest mind the same transcendent destiny; and not minors and invalids in a protected corner, not cowards fleeing before a revolution, but guides, redeemers and benefactors, obeying the Almighty effort and advancing on Chaos and the Dark.

What pretty oracles nature yields us on this text in the face and behavior of children, babes, and even brutes! That divided and rebel mind, that distrust of a sentiment because our arithmetic has computed the strength and means opposed to our purpose, these have not. Their mind being whole, their eye is as yet unconquered, and when we look in their faces we are disconcerted. Infancy conforms to nobody; all conform to it; so that one babe commonly makes four or five out of the adults who prattle and play to it. So God has armed youth and puberty and manhood no less with its own piquancy and charm, and made it enviable and gracious and its claims not to be put by, if it will stand by itself. Do not think the youth has no force, because he cannot speak to you and me. Hark! in the next room his voice is sufficiently clear and emphatic. It seems he knows how to speak to his contemporaries. Bashful or bold then, he will know how to make us seniors very unnecessary.

The nonchalance of boys who are sure of a dinner, and would disdain as much as a lord to do or say aught to conciliate one, is the healthy attitude of human nature. A boy is in the parlor what the pit is in the playhouse; independent, irresponsible, looking out from his corner on such people and facts as pass by, he tries and sentences them on their merits, in the swift, summary way of boys, as good, bad, interesting, silly, eloquent, troublesome. He cumbers himself never about consequences, about interests; he gives an independent, genuine verdict. You must court him; he does not court you. But the man is as it were clapped into jail by his consciousness. As soon as he has once acted or spoken with éclat he is a committed person, watched by the sympathy or the hatred of hundreds, whose affections must now enter into his account. There is no Lethe for this. Ah, that he could pass again into his neutrality! Who can thus avoid all pledges and, having observed, observe again from the same unaffected, unbiased, unbribable, unaffrighted innocence,—must always be formidable. He

would utter opinions on all passing affairs,
which being seen to be not private but necessary, would sink like darts into the ear of men
and put them in fear.

These are the voices which we hear in solitude, but they grow faint and inaudible as we
enter into the world. Society everywhere is in
conspiracy against the manhood of every one
of its members. Society is a joint-stock company,
in which the members agree, for the better se-
curing of his bread to each shareholder, to sur-
render the liberty and culture of the eater. The
virtue in most request is conformity. Self-
reliance is its aversion. It loves not realities and
creators, but names and customs.

Whoso would be a man, must be a nonconform-
ist. He who would gather immortal palms must
not be hindered by the name of goodness, but
must explore if it be goodness. Nothing is at
last sacred but the integrity of your own mind.
Absolve you to yourself, and you shall have the
suffrage of the world. I remember an answer
which when quite young I was prompted to
make to a valued adviser who was wont to
importune me with the dear old doctrines of the
church. On my saying, "What have I to do with
the sacredness of traditions, if I live wholly from
within?" my friend suggested,—"But these im-
pulses may be from below, not from above."
I replied, "They do not seem to me to be such;
but if I am the Devil's child, I will live then
from the Devil." No law can be sacred to me
but that of my nature. Good and bad are but

names very readily transferable to that or this;
the only right is what is after my constitution;
the only wrong what is against it. A man is to
carry himself in the presence of all opposition
as if every thing were titular and ephemeral but
he. I am ashamed to think how easily we capitu-
late to badges and names, to large societies and
dead institutions. Every decent and well-spoken
individual affects and sways me more than is
right. I ought to go upright and vital, and speak
the rude truth in all ways. If malice and vanity
wear the coat of philanthropy, shall that pass?
If an angry bigot assumes this bountiful cause
of Abolition, and comes to me with his last news
from Barbadoes, why should I not say to him,
'Go love thy infant; love thy wood-chopper; be
good-natured and modest; have that grace; and
never varnish your hard, uncharitable ambition
with this incredible tenderness for black folk
a thousand miles off. Thy love afar is spite at
home.' Rough and graceless would be such
greeting, but truth is handsomer than the affectation of love. Your goodness must have some
edge to it,—else it is none. The doctrine of hatred
must be preached, as the counteraction of the
doctrine of love, when that pules and whines.
I shun father and mother and wife and brother
when my genius calls me. I would write on the
lintels of the door-post, *Whim.* I hope it is somewhat better than whim at last, but we cannot
spend the day in explanation. Expect me not
to show cause why I seek or why I exclude
company. Then again, do not tell me, as a good

man did to-day, of my obligation to put all poor men in good situations. Are they *my* poor? I tell thee, thou foolish philanthropist, that I grudge the dollar, the dime, the cent I give to such men as do not belong to me and to whom I do not belong. There is a class of persons to whom by all spiritual affinity I am bought and sold; for them I will go to prison if need be; but your miscellaneous popular charities; the education at college of fools; the building of meeting-houses to the vain end to which many now stand; alms to sots, and the thousand-fold Relief Societies;—though I confess with shame I sometimes succumb and give the dollar, it is a wicked dollar, which by and by I shall have the manhood to withhold.

Virtues are, in the popular estimate, rather the exception than the rule. There is the man *and* his virtues. Men do what is called a good action, as some piece of courage or charity, much as they would pay a fine in expiation of daily non-appearance on parade. Their works are done as an apology or extenuation of their living in the world,—as invalids and the insane pay a high board. Their virtues are penances. I do not wish to expiate, but to live. My life is for itself and not for a spectacle. I much prefer that it should be of a lower strain, so it be genuine and equal, than that it should be glittering and unsteady. I wish it to be sound and sweet, and not to need diet and bleeding. I ask primary evidence that you are a man, and refuse this appeal from the man to his actions. I know that for myself it makes no difference whether I do or forbear those actions which are reckoned excellent. I cannot consent to pay for a privilege where I have intrinsic right. Few and mean as my gifts may be, I actually am, and do not need for my own assurance or the assurance of my fellows any secondary testimony.

What I must do is all that concerns me, not what the people think. This rule, equally arduous in actual and in intellectual life, may serve for the whole distinction between greatness and meanness. It is the harder because you will always find those who think they know what is your duty better than you know it. It is easy in the world to live after the world's opinion; it is easy in solitude to live after our own; but the great man is he who in the midst of the crowd keeps with perfect sweetness the independence of solitude.

The objection to conforming to usages that have become dead to you is that it scatters your force. It loses your time and blurs the impression of your character. If you maintain a dead church, contribute to a dead Bible-society, vote with a great party either for the government or against it, spread your table like base housekeepers,—under all these screens I have difficulty to detect the precise man you are: and of course so much force is withdrawn from your proper life. But do your work, and I shall know you. Do your work, and you shall reinforce yourself. A man must consider what a blind-man's-buff is this game of conformity. If I know

your sect I anticipate your argument. I hear a
preacher announce for his text and topic the
expediency of one of the institutions of his
church. Do I not know beforehand that not possibly can he say a new and spontaneous word?
Do I not know that with all this ostentation of
examining the grounds of the institution he will
do no such thing? Do I not know that he is
pledged to himself not to look but at one side,
the permitted side, not as a man, but as a parish
minister? He is a retained attorney, and these
airs of the bench are the emptiest affectation.
Well, most men have bound their eyes with one
or another handkerchief, and attached themselves to some one of these communities of
opinion. This conformity makes them not false
in a few particulars, authors of a few lies, but
false in all particulars. Their every truth is not
quite true. Their two is not the real two, their
four not the real four; so that every word they
say chagrins us and we know not where to begin
to set them right. Meantime nature is not slow
to equip us in the prison-uniform of the party
to which we adhere. We come to wear one cut
of face and figure, and acquire by degrees the
gentlest asinine expression. There is a mortify-
ing experience in particular, which does not fail
to wreak itself also in the general history; I mean
"the foolish face of praise," the forced smile
which we put on in company where we do not
feel at ease, in answer to conversation which
does not interest us. The muscles, not sponta-
neously moved but moved by a low usurping

wilfulness, grow tight about the outline of the face, with the most disagreeable sensation.

For nonconformity the world whips you with its displeasure. And therefore a man must know how to estimate a sour face. The by-standers look askance on him in the public street or in the friend's parlor. If this aversion had its origin in contempt and resistance like his own he might well go home with a sad countenance; but the sour faces of the multitude, like their sweet faces, have no deep cause, but are put on and off as the wind blows and a newspaper directs. Yet is the discontent of the multitude more formidable than that of the senate and the college. It is easy enough for a firm man who knows the world to brook the rage of the cultivated classes. Their rage is decorous and prudent, for they are timid, as being very vulnerable themselves. But when to their feminine rage the indignation of the people is added, when the ignorant and the poor are aroused, when the unintelligent brute force that lies at the bottom of society is made to growl and mow, it needs the habit of magnanimity and religion to treat it godlike as a trifle of no concernment.

The other terror that scares us from self-trust is our consistency; a reverence for our past act or word because the eyes of others have no other data for computing our orbit than our past acts, and we are loth to disappoint them.

But why should you keep your head over your shoulder? Why drag about this corpse of your memory, lest you contradict somewhat you have

stated in this or that public place? Suppose you
should contradict yourself; what then? It seems
to be a rule of wisdom never to rely on your
memory alone, scarcely even in acts of pure
memory, but to bring the past for judgment into
the thousand-eyed present, and live ever in a
new day. In your metaphysics you have denied
personality to the Deity, yet when the devout
motions of the soul come, yield to them heart
and life, though they should clothe God with
shape and color. Leave your theory, as Joseph
his coat in the hand of the harlot, and flee.

A foolish consistency is the hobgoblin of little
minds, adored by little statesmen and philoso-
phers and divines. With consistency a great soul
has simply nothing to do. He may as well con-
cern himself with his shadow on the wall. Speak
what you think now in hard words and tomorrow speak what to-morrow thinks in hard words
again, though it contradict everything you said
to-day.—'Ah, so you shall be sure to be misunderstood.'—Is it so bad then to be misunderstood? Pythagoras was misunderstood, and
Socrates, and Jesus, and Luther, and Copernicus,
and Galileo, and Newton, and every pure and
wise spirit that ever took flesh. To be great is
to be misunderstood.

I suppose no man can violate his nature. All
the sallies of his will are rounded in by the law
of his being, as the inequalities of Andes and
Himmaleh are insignificant in the curve of the
sphere. Nor does it matter how you gauge and
try him. A character is like an acrostic or Alex-

andrian stanza;—read it forward, backward, or across, it still spells the same thing. In this pleasing contrite wood-life which God allows me, let me record day by day my honest thought without prospect or retrospect, and, I cannot doubt, it will be found symmetrical, though I mean it not and see it not. My book should smell of pines and resound with the hum of insects. The swallow over my window should interweave that thread or straw he carries in his bill into my web also. We pass for what we are. Character teaches above our wills. Men imagine that they communicate their virtue or vice only by overt actions, and do not see that virtue or vice emit a breath every moment.

There will be an agreement in whatever variety of actions, so they be each honest and natural in their hour. For of one will, the actions will be harmonious, however unlike they seem. These varieties are lost sight of at a little distance, at a little height of thought. One tendency unites them all. The voyage of the best ship is a zigzag line of a hundred tacks. See the line from a sufficient distance, and it straightens itself to the average tendency. Your genuine action will explain itself and will explain your other genuine actions. Your conformity explains nothing. Act singly, and what you have already done singly will justify you now. Greatness appeals to the future. If I can be firm enough to-day to do right and scorn eyes, I must have done so much right before as to defent me now. Be it how it will, do right now. Always scorn appearances and you always may. The force of character is cumulative. All the foregone days of virtue work their health into this. What makes the majesty of the heroes of the senate and the field, which so fills the imagination? The consciousness of a train of great days and victories behind. They shed a united light on the advancing actor. He is attended as by a visible escort of angels. That is it which throws thunder into Chatham's voice, and dignity into Washington's port, and America into Adams's eye. Honor is venerable to us because it is no ephemera. It is always ancient virtue. We worship it to-day because it is not of today. We love it and pay it homage because it is not a trap for our love and homage, but is self-dependent, self-derived, and therefore of an old immaculate pedigree, even if shown in a young person.

I hope in these days we have heard the last of conformity and consistency. Let the words be gazetted and ridiculous henceforward. Instead of the gong for dinner, let us hear a whistle from the Spartan fife. Let us never bow and apologize more. A great man is coming to eat at my house. I do not wish to please him; I wish that he should wish to please me. I will stand here for humanity, and though I would make it kind, I would make it true. Let us affront and reprimand the smooth mediocrity and squalid contentment of the times, and hurl in the face of custom and trade and office, the fact which is the upshot of all history, that there is a great responsible Thinker and Actor working wherever a man works; that a true man belongs to no other time or place, but is the centre of things. Where he is, there is nature. He measures you and all men and all events. Ordinarily, every body in society reminds us of somewhat else, or of some other person. Character, reality, reminds you of nothing else; it takes place of the whole creation. The man must be so much that he must make all circumstances indifferent. Every true man is a cause, a country, and an age; requires infinite spaces and numbers and time fully to accomplish his design;—and posterity seem to follow his steps as a train of clients. A man Caesar is born, and for ages after we have a Roman Empire. Christ is born, and millions of minds so grow and cleave to his genius that he is confounded with virtue and the possible of man. An institution is the lengthened shadow of one man; as, Monachism, of the Hermit Antony; the Reformation, of Luther; Quakerism, of Fox; Methodism, of Wesley; Abolition, of Clarkson. Scipio, Milton called "the height of Rome"; and all history resolves itself very easily into the biography of a few stout and earnest persons.

Let a man then know his worth, and keep things under his feet. Let him not peep or steal, or skulk up and down with the air of a charity-boy, a bastard, or an interloper in the world which exists for him. But the man in the street, finding no worth in himself which corresponds to the force which built a tower or sculptured a marble god, feels poor when he looks on these.

To him a palace, a statue, or a costly book have an alien and forbidding air, much like a gay equipage, and seem to say like that, "Who are you, Sir?" Yet they all are his, suitors for his notice, petitioners to his faculties that they will come out and take possession. The picture waits for my verdict; it is not to command me, but I am to settle its claims to praise. That popular fable of the sot who was picked up dead-drunk in the street, carried to the duke's house, washed and dressed and laid in the duke's bed, and, on his waking, treated with all obsequious ceremony like the duke, and assured that he had been insane, owes its popularity to the fact that it symbolizes so well the state of man, who is in the world a sort of sot, but now and then wakes up, exercises his reason and finds himself a true prince.

Our reading is mendicant and sycophantic. In history our imagination plays us false. Kingdom and lordship, power and estate, are a gaudier vocabulary than private John and Edward in a small house and common day's work; but the things of life are the same to both; the sum total of both is the same. Why all this deference to Alfred and Scanderberg and Gustavus? Suppose they were virtuous; did they wear out virtue? As great a stake depends on your private act to-day as followed their public and renowned steps. When private men shall act with original views, the lustre will be transferred from the actions of kings to those of gentlemen.

The world has been instructed by its kings, who have so magnetized the eyes of nations.

It has been taught by this colossal symbol the mutual reverence that is due from man to man. The joyful loyalty with which men have everywhere suffered the king, the noble, or the great proprietor to walk among them by a law of his own, make his own scale of men and things and reverse theirs, pay for benefits not with money but with honor, and represent the law in his person, was the hieroglyphic by which they obscurely signified their consciousness of their own right and comeliness, the right of every man.

The magnetism which all original action exerts is explained when we inquire the reason of self-trust. Who is the Trustee? What is the aboriginal Self, on which a universal reliance may be grounded? What is the nature and power of that science-baffling star, without parallax, without calculable elements, which shoots a ray of beauty even into trivial and impure actions, if the least mark of independence appear? The inquiry leads us to that source, at once the essence of genius, of virtue, and of life, which we call Spontaneity or Instinct. We denote this primary wisdom as Intuition, whilst all later teachings are tuitions. In that deep force, the last fact behind which analysis cannot go, all things find their common origin. For the sense of being which in calm hours rises, we know not how, in the soul, is not diverse from things, from space, from light, from time, from man, but one with them and proceeds obviously from the same source whence their life and being also proceed. We first share the life by which things exist and afterwards see them as appearances in nature and forget that we have shared their cause. Here is the fountain of action and of thought. Here are the lungs of that inspiration which giveth man wisdom and which cannot be denied without impiety and atheism. We lie in the lap of immense intelligence, which makes us receivers of its truth and organs of its activity. When we discern justice, when we discern truth, we do nothing of ourselves, but allow a passage to its beams. If we ask whence this comes, if we seek to pry into the soul that causes, all philosophy is at fault. Its presence or its absence is all we can affirm. Every man discriminates between the voluntary acts of his mind and his involuntary perceptions, and knows that to his involuntary perceptions a perfect faith is due. He may err in the expression of them, but he knows that these things are so, like day and night, not to be disputed. My wilful actions and acquisitions are but roving;—the idlest reverie, the faintest native emotion, command my curiosity and respect. Thoughtless people contradict as readily the statement of perceptions as of opinions, or rather much more readily; for they do not distinguish between perception and notion. They fancy that I choose to see this or that thing. But perception is not whimsical, but fatal. If I see a trait, my children will see it after me, and in course of time all mankind,—although it may chance that no one has seen it before me. For my perception of it is as much a fact as the sun.

The relations of the soul to the divine spirit are so pure that it is profane to seek to interpose helps. It must be that when God speaketh he should communicate, not one thing, but all things; should fill the world with his voice; should scatter forth light, nature, time, souls, from the centre of the present thought; and new date and new create the whole. Whenever a mind is simple and receives a divine wisdom, old things pass away,—means, teachers, texts, temples fall; it lives now, and absorbs past and future in the present hour. All things are made sacred by relation to it,—one as much as another. All things are dissolved to their centre by their cause, and in the universal miracle petty and particular miracles disappear. If therefore a man claims to know and speak of God and carries you backward to the phraseology of some old mouldered nation in another country, in another world, believe him not. Is the acorn better than the oak which is its fulness and completion? Is the parent better than the child into whom he has cast his ripened being? Whence then this worship of the past? The centuries are conspirators against the sanity and authority of the soul. Time and space are but physiological colors which the eye makes, but the soul is light: where it is, is day; where it was, is night; and history is an impertinence and an injury if it be any thing more than a cheerful apologue or parable of my being and becoming.

Man is timid and apologetic; he is no longer upright; he dares not say 'I think,' 'I am,' but

quotes some saint or sage. He is ashamed before
the blade of grass or the blowing rose. These
roses under my window make no reference to
former roses or to better ones; they are for what
they are; they exist with God to-day. There is
no time to them. There is simply the rose; it
is perfect in every moment of its existence. Before a leaf-bud has burst, its whole life acts;
in the full-blown flower there is no more; in
the leafless root there is no less. Its nature is
satisfied and it satisfies nature in all moments
alike. But man postpones or remembers; he does
not live in the present, but with reverted eye
laments the past, or, heedless of the riches that
surround him, stands on tiptoe to foresee the
future. He cannot be happy and strong until he
too lives with nature in the present, above time.

This should be plain enough. Yet see what
strong intellects dare not yet hear God himself
unless he speak the phraseology of I know not
what David, or Jeremiah, or Paul. We shall not
always set so great a price on a few texts, on
a few lives. We are like children who repeat
by rote the sentences of grandames and tutors,
and, as they grow older, of the men of talents
and character they chance to see,—painfully rec-
ollecting the exact words they spoke; afterwards, when they come into the point of view
which those had who uttered these sayings, they
understand them and are willing to let the words
go; for at any time they can use words as good
when occasion comes. If we live truly, we shall
see truly. It is as easy for the strong man to

be strong, as it is for the weak to be weak. When we have new perception, we shall gladly disburden the memory of its hoarded treasures as old rubbish. When a man lives with God, his voice shall be as sweet as the murmur of the brook and the rustle of the corn.

And now at last the highest truth on this subject remains unsaid; probably cannot be said; for all that we say is the far-off remembering of the intuition. That thought by what I can now nearest approach to say it, is this. When good is near you, when you have life in yourself, it is not by any known or accustomed way; you shall not discern the footprints of any other; you shall not see the face of man; you shall not hear any name;—the way, the thought, the good, shall be wholly strange and new. It shall exclude example and experience. You take the way from man, not to man. All persons that ever existed are its forgotten ministers. Fear and hope are alike beneath it. There is somewhat low even in hope. In the hour of vision there is nothing that can be called gratitude, nor properly joy. The soul raised over passion beholds identity and eternal causation, perceives the self-existence of Truth and Right, and calms itself with knowing that all things go well. Vast spaces of nature, the Atlantic Ocean, the South Sea; long intervals of time, years, centuries, are of no account. This which I think and feel underlay every former state of life and circumstances, as it does underlie my present, and what is called life and what is called death.

Life only avails, not the having lived. Power ceases in the instant of repose; it resides in the moment of transition from a past to a new state, in the shooting of the gulf, in the darting to an aim. This one fact the world hates; that the soul *becomes;* for that forever degrades the past, turns all riches to poverty, all reputation to shame, confounds the saint with the rogue, shoves Jesus and Judas equally aside. Why then do we prate of self-reliance? Inasmuch as the soul is present there will be power not confident but agent. To talk of reliance is a poor external way of speaking. Speak rather of that which relies because it works and is. Who has more obedience than I masters me, though he should not raise his finger. Round him I must revolve by the gravitation of spirits. We fancy it rhetoric when we speak of eminent virtue. We do not yet see that virtue is Height, and that a man or a company of men, plastic and permeable to principles, by the law of nature must overpower and ride all cities, nations, kings, rich men, poets, who are not.

This is the ultimate fact which we so quickly reach on this, as on every topic, the resolution of all into the ever-blessed ONE. Self-existence is the attribute of the Supreme Cause, and it constitutes the measure of good by the degree in which it enters into all lower forms. All things real are so by so much virtue as they contain. Commerce, husbandry, hunting, whaling, war, eloquence, personal weight, are somewhat, and engage my respect as examples of its presence and impure action. I see the same law working in nature for conservation and growth. Power is, in nature, the essential measure of right. Nature suffers nothing to remain in her kingdoms which cannot help itself. The genesis and maturation of a planet, its poise and orbit, the bended tree recovering itself from the strong wind, the vital resources of every animal and vegetable, are demonstrations of the self-sufficing and therefore self-relying soul.

Thus all concentrates: let us not rove; let us sit at home with the cause. Let us stun and astonish the intruding rabble of men and books and institutions by a simple declaration of the divine fact. Bid the invaders take the shoes from off their feet, for God is here within. Let our simplicity judge them, and our docility to our own law demonstrate the poverty of nature and fortune beside our native riches.

But now we are a mob. Man does not stand in awe of man, nor is his genius admonished to stay at home, to put itself in communication with the internal ocean, but it goes abroad to beg a cup of water of the urns of other men. We must go alone. I like the silent church before the service begins, better than any preaching. How far off, how cool, how chaste the persons look, begirt each one with a precinct or sanctuary! So let us always sit. Why should we assume the faults of our friend, or wife, or father, or child, because they sit around our hearth, or are said to have the same blood? All men have my blood and I all men's. Not for that will I adopt

their petulance or folly, even to the extent of
being ashamed of it. But your isolation must not
be mechanical, but spiritual, that is, must be
elevation. At times the whole world seems to
be in conspiracy to importune you with emphatic trifles. Friend, client, child, sickness, fear,
want, charity, all knock at once at thy closet
door and say,—'Come out unto us.' But keep thy
state; come not into their confusion. The power
men possess to annoy me I give them by a weak
curiosity. No man can come near me but through
my act. "What we love that we have, but by
desire we bereave ourselves of the love."

If we cannot at once rise to the sanctities of
obedience and faith, let us at least resist our
temptations; let us enter into the state of war
and wake Thor and Woden, courage and con-
stancy, in our Saxon breasts. This is to be done
in our smooth times by speaking the truth.
Check this lying hospitality and lying affection.
Live no longer to the expectation of these de-
ceived and deceiving people with whom we
converse. Say to them, 'O father, O mother, O
wife, O brother, O friend, I have lived with you
after appearances hitherto. Henceforward I am
the truth's. Be it known unto you that henceforward I obey no law less than the external
law. I will have no covenants but proximities.
I shall endeavor to nourish my parents, to support my family, to be the chaste husband of one
wife,—but these relations I must fill after a new
and unprecedented way. I appeal from your
customs. I must be myself. I cannot break myself

any longer for you, or you. If you can love me for what I am, we shall be the happier. If you cannot, I will still seek to deserve that you should. I will not hide my tastes or aversions. I will so trust that what is deep is holy, that I will do strongly before the sun and moon whatever inly rejoices me and the heart appoints. If you are noble, I will love you; if you are not, I will not hurt you and myself by hypocritical attentions. If you are true, but not in the same truth with me, cleave to your companions; I will seek my own. I do this not selfishly but humbly and truly. It is alike your interest, and mine, and all men's however long we have dwelt in lies, to live in truth. Does this sound harsh to-day? You will soon love what is dictated by your nature as well as mine, and if we follow the truth it will bring us out safe at last.'—But so may you give these friends pain. Yes, but I cannot sell my liberty and my power, to save their sensibility. Besides, all persons have their moments of reason, when they look out into the region of absolute truth; then will they justify me and do the same thing.

The populace think that your rejection of popular standards is a rejection of all standard, and mere antinomianism; and the bold sensualist will use the name of philosophy to gild his crimes. But the law of consciousness abides. There are two confessionals, in one or the other of which we must be shriven. You may fulfil your round of duties by clearing yourself in the *direct*, or in the *reflex* way. Consider whether

you have satisfied your relations to father,
mother, cousin, neighbor, town, cat and dog—
whether any of these can upbraid you. But I
may also neglect this reflex standard and absolve me to myself. I have my own stern claims
and perfect circle. It denies the name of duty
to many offices that are called duties. But if I
can discharge its debts it enables me to dispense
with the popular code. If any one imagines that
this law is lax, let him keep its commandment
one day.

And truly it demands something godlike in
him who has cast off the common motives of
humanity and has ventured to trust himself for
a taskmaster. High be his heart, faithful his will,
clear his sight, that he may in good earnest be
doctrine, society, law, to himself, that a simple
purpose may be to him as strong as iron necessity is to others!

If any man consider the present aspects of
what is called by distinction *society*, he will see
the need of these ethics. The sinew and heart
of man seem to be drawn out, and we are become timorous, desponding whimperers. We are
afraid of truth, afraid of fortune, afraid of death,
and afraid of each other. Out age yields no great
and perfect persons. We want men and women
who shall renovate life and our social state, but
we see that most natures are insolvent, cannot
satisfy their own wants, have an ambition out
of all proportion to their practical force and do
lean and beg day and night continually. Our
housekeeping is mendicant, our arts, our occu-

pations, our marriages, our religion we have not chosen, but society has chosen for us. We are parlor soldiers. We shun the rugged battle of fate, where strength is born.

If our young men miscarry in their first enterprises they lose all heart. If the young merchant fails, men say he is *ruined*. If the finest genius studies at one of our colleges and is not installed in an office within one year afterwards in the cities or suburbs of Boston or New York, it seems to his friends and to himself that he is right in being disheartened and in complaining the rest of his life. A sturdy lad from New Hampshire or Vermont, who in turn tries all the professions, who *teams it, farms it, peddles*, keeps a school, preaches, edits a newspaper, goes to Congress, buys a township, and so forth, in successive years, and always like a cat falls on his feet, is worth a hundred of these city dolls. He walks abreast with his days and feels no shame in not 'studying a profession,' for he does not postpone his life, but lives already. He has not one chance, but a hundred chances. Let a Stoic open the resources of man and tell men they are not leaning willows, but can and must detach themselves; that with the exercise of self-trust, new powers shall appear; that a man is the word made flesh, born to shed healing to the nations; that he should be ashamed of our compassion, and that the moment he acts from himself, tossing the laws, the books, idolatries and customs out of the window, we pity him no more but thank and revere him;—and that teacher shall restore the life of man to splendor and make his name dear to all history.

It is easy to see that a greater self-reliance must work a revolution in all the offices and relations of men; in their religion; in their education; in their pursuits; their modes of living; their association; in their property; in their speculative views.

In what prayers do men allow themselves! That which they call a holy office is not so much as brave and manly. Prayer looks abroad and asks for some foreign addition to come through some foreign virtue, and loses itself in endless mazes of natural and supernatural, and mediatorial and miraculous. Prayer that craves a particular commodity, anything less than all good, is vicious. Prayer is the contemplation of the facts of life from the highest point of view. It is the soliloquy of a beholding and jubilant soul. It is the spirit of God pronouncing his works good. But prayer as a means to effect a private end is meanness and theft. It supposes dualism and not unity in nature and consciousness. As soon as the man is at one with God, he will not beg. He will then see prayer in all action. The prayer of the farmer kneeling in his field to weed it, the prayer of the rower kneeling with the stroke of his oar, his true prayers heard throughout nature, though for cheap ends. Caratach, in Fletcher's "Bonduca," when admonished to inquire the mind of the god Audate, replies,—

"His hidden meaning lies in our endeavors;

Our valors are our best gods."

Another sort of false prayers are our regrets. Discontent is the want of self-reliance: it is infirmity of will. Regret calamities if you can thereby help the sufferer; if not, attend your own work and already the evil begins to be repaired. Our sympathy is just as base. We come to them who weep foolishly and sit down and cry for company, instead of imparting to them truth and health in rough electric shocks, putting them once more in communication with their own reason. The secret of fortune is joy in our hands. Welcome evermore to gods and men is the self-helping man. For him all doors are flung wide; him all tongues greet, all honors crown, all eyes follow with desire. Our love goes out to him and embraces him because he did not need it. We solicitously and apologetically caress and celebrate him because he held on his way and scorned our disapprobation. The gods love him because men hated him. "To the persevering mortal," said Zoroaster, "the blessed Immortals are swift."

As men's prayers are a disease of the will, so are their creeds a disease of the intellect. They say with those foolish Israelites, 'Let not God speak to us, lest we die. Speak thou, speak any man with us, and we will obey.' Everywhere I am hindered of meeting God in my brother, because he has shut his own temple doors and recites fables merely of his brother's, or his brother's brother's God. Every new mind is a new classification. If it prove a mind of uncommon activity and power, a Locke, a Lavoisier, a Hutton, a Bentham, a Fourier, it imposes its classification on other men, and lo! a new system. In proportion to the depth of the thought, and so to the number of the objects it touches and brings within reach of the pupil, is his complacency. But chiefly is this apparent in creeds and churches, which are also classifications of some powerful mind acting on the elemental thought of duty and man's relation to the Highest. Such is Calvinism, Quakerism, Swedenborgism. The pupil takes the same delight in subordinating every thing to the new terminology as a girl who has just learned botany in seeing a new earth and new seasons thereby. It will happen for a time that the pupil will find his intellectual power has grown by the study of his master's mind. But in all unbalanced minds the classification is idolized, passes for the end and not for a speedily exhaustible means, so that the walls of the system blend to their eye in the remote horizon with the walls of the universe; the luminaries of heaven seem to them hung on the arch their master built. They cannot imagine how you aliens have any right to see,— how you can see; 'It must be somehow that you stole the light from us.' They do not yet perceive that light, unsystematic, indomitable, will break into any cabin, even into theirs. Let them chirp awhile and call it their own. If they are honest and do well, presently their neat new pinfold will be too strait and low, will crack, will lean, will rot and vanish, and the immortal light, all young and joyful, million-orbed, million-colored, will beam over the universe as on the first morning.

It is for want of self-culture that the superstition of Travelling, whose idols are Italy, England, Egypt, retains its fascination for all educated Americans. They who made England, Italy, or Greece venerable in the imagination, did so by sticking fast where they were, like an axis of the earth. In manly hours we feel that duty is our place. The soul is no traveller; the wise man stays at home, and when his necessities, his duties, on any occasion call him from his house, or into foreign lands, he is at home still and shall make men sensible by the expression of his countenance that he goes, the missionary of wisdom and virtue, and visits cities and men like a sovereign and not like an interloper or a valet.

I have no churlish objection to the circumnavigation of the globe for the purposes of art, of study, and benevolence, so that the man is first domesticated, or does not go abroad with the hope of finding somewhat greater than he knows. He who travels to be amused, or to get somewhat which he does not carry, travels away from himself, and grows old even in youth among old things. In Thebes, in Palmyra, his will and mind have become old and dilapidated as they. He carries ruins to ruins.

Travelling is a fool's paradise. Our first journeys discover to us the indifference of places. At home I dream that at Naples, at Rome, I can be intoxicated with beauty and lose my sadness. I pack my trunk, embrace my friends, embark on the sea and at last wake up in Naples, and there beside me is the stern fact, the sad self, unrelenting, identical, that I fled from. I seek the Vatican and the palaces. I affect to be intoxicated with sights and suggestions, but I am not intoxicated. My giant goes with me wherever I go.

But the rage of travelling is a symptom of a deeper unsoundness affecting the whole intellectual action. The intellect is vagabond, and our system of education fosters restlessness. Our minds travel when our bodies are forced to stay at home. We imitate; and what is imitation but the travelling of the mind? Our houses are built with foreign taste; our shelves are garnished with foreign ornaments; our opinions, our tastes, our faculties, lean, and follow the Past and the Distant. The soul created the arts wherever they have flourished. It was in his own mind that the artist sought his model. It was an application of his own thought to the thing to be done and the conditions to be observed. And why need we copy the Doric or the Gothic model? Beauty, convenience, grandeur of thought and quaint expression are as near to us as to any, and if the American artist will study with hope and love the precise thing to be done by him, considering the climate, the soil, the length of the day, the wants of the people, the habit and form of the government, he will create a house in which all these will find themselves fitted, and taste and sentiment will be satisfied also.

Insist on yourself; never imitate. Your own gift you can present every moment with the cumulative force of a whole life's cultivation; but of the adopted talent of another you have only an extemporaneous half possession. That which each can do best, none but his Maker can teach him. No man yet knows what it is, nor can, till that person has exhibited it. Where is the master who could have taught Shakespeare? Where is the master who could have instructed Franklin, or Washington, or Bacon, or Newton? Every great man is unique. The Scipionism of Scipio is precisely that part he could not borrow. Shakespeare will never be made by the study of Shakespeare. Do that which is assigned you, and you cannot hope too much or dare too much. There is at this moment for you an utterance brave and grand as that of the colossal chisel of Phidias, or trowel of the Egyptians, or the pen of Moses or Dante, but different from all these. Not possibly will the soul, all rich, all eloquent, with thousand-cloven tongue, deign to repeat itself; but if you can hear what these patriarchs say, surely you can reply to them in the same pitch of voice; for the ear and the tongue are two organs of one nature. Abide in the simple and noble regions of thy life, obey thy heart, and thou shalt reproduce the Foreworld again.

As our Religion, our Education, our Art look abroad, so does our spirit of society. All men plume themselves on the improvement of society, and no man improves.

Society never advances. It recedes as fast on one side as it gains on the other. It undergoes continual changes; it is barbarous, it is civilized, it is Christianized, it is rich, it is scientific; but this change is not amelioration. For everything that is given something is taken. Society acquires new arts and loses old instincts. What a contrast between the well-clad, reading, writing, thinking American, with a watch, a pencil and a bill of exchange in his pocket, and the naked New Zealander, whose property is a club, a spear, a mat and an undivided twentieth of a shed to sleep under! But compare the health of the two men and you shall see that the white man has lost his aboriginal strength. If the traveller tell us truly, strike the savage with a broad-axe and in a day or two the flesh shall unite and heal as if you struck the blow into soft pitch, and the same blow shall send the white to his grave.

The civilized man has built a coach, but has lost the use of his feet. He is supported on crutches, but lacks so much support of muscle. He has a fine Geneva watch, but he fails of the skill to tell the hour by the sun. A Greenwich nautical almanac he has, and so being sure of the information when he wants it, the man in the street does not know a star in the sky. The solstice he does not observe; the equinox he knows as little; and the whole bright calendar of the year is without a dial in his mind. His note-books impair his memory; his libraries overload his wit; the insurance-office increases the number of accidents; and it may be a question whether machinery does not encumber, whether we have not lost by refinement some energy, by a Christianity, entrenched in establishments and forms, some vigor of wild virtue. For every Stoic was a Stoic; but in Christendom where is the Christian?

There is no more deviation in the moral standard than in the standard of height or bulk. No greater men are now than ever were. A singular equality may be observed between the great men of the first and of the last ages; nor can all the science, art, religion, and philosophy of the nineteenth century avail to educate greater men than Plutarch's heroes, three or four and twenty centuries ago. Not in time is the race progressive. Phocion, Socrates, Anaxagoras, Diogenes, are great men, but they leave no class. He who is really of their class will not be called by their name, but will be his own man, and in his turn the founder of a sect. The arts and inventions of each period are only its costume and do not invigorate men. The harm of the improved machinery may compensate its good. Hudson and Behring accomplished so much in their fishing-boats as to astonish Parry and Franklin, whose equipment exhausted the resources of science and art. Galileo, with an operaglass, discovered a more splendid series of celestial phenomena than any one since. Columbus found the New World in an undecked boat. It is curious to see the periodical disuse and perishing of means and machinery which were introduced with loud laudation a few years or centuries before. The great genius returns to essential man. We reckoned the improvements of the art of war among the triumphs of science, and yet Napoleon conquered Europe by the bivouac, which consisted of falling back on naked valor and disencumbering it of all aids. The Emperor held it impossible to make a perfect army, says Las Cases, "without abolishing our arms, magazines, commissaries, and carriages, until, in imitation of the Roman custom, the soldier should receive his supply of corn, grind it in his hand-mill and bake his bread himself."

Society is a wave. The wave oves onward, but the water of which it is composed does not. The same particle does not rise from the valley to the ridge. Its unity is only phenomenal. The persons who make up a nation to-day, next year die, and their experience dies with them.

And so the reliance on Property, including the reliance on governments which protect it, is the want of self-reliance. Men have looked away from themselves and at things so long that they have come to esteem the religious, learned and civil institutions as guards of property, and they deprecate assaults on these, because they feel them to be assaults on property. They measure their esteem of each other by what each has, and not by what each is. But a cultivated man becomes ashamed of his property, out of new respect for his nature. Especially he hates what he has if he sees that it is accidental,—came to him by inheritance, or gift, or crime; then he feels that it is not having; it does not belong to him, has no root in him and merely lies there because no revolution or no robber takes it away. But what which a man is, does always by necessity acquire; and what the man acquires, is living property, which does not wait the beck of rulers, or mobs, or revolutions, or fire, or storm, or bankruptcies, but perpetually renews itself wherever the man breathes. "Thy lot or portion of life," said the Caliph Ali, "is seeking after thee; therefore be at rest from seeking after it." Our dependence on these foreign goods leads us to our slavish respect for numbers. The political parties meet in numerous conventions; the greater the concourse and with each new uproar of announcement, The Delegation from Essex! The Democrats from New Hampshire! The Whigs of Maine! the young patriot feels himself stronger than before by a new thousand of eyes and arms. In like manner the reformers summon conventions and vote and resolve in multitude. Not so, O friends! will the God deign to enter and inhabit you, but by a method precisely the reverse. It is only as a man puts off all foreign support and stands alone that I see him to be strong and to prevail. He is weaker by every recruit to his banner. Is not a man better than a town? Ask nothing of men, and, in the endless mutation, thou only firm column must presently appear the upholder of all that surrounds thee. He who knows that power is inborn, that he is weak because he has looked for good out of him and elsewhere, and, so perceiving, throws himself unhesitatingly on his thought, instantly rights himself, stands in the erect position, commands his limbs, works miracles; just as a man who stands on his feet is stronger than a man who stands on his head.

So use all that is called Fortune. Most men gamble with her, and gain all, and lose all, as her wheel rolls. But do thou leave as unlawful these winnings, and deal with Cause and Effect, the chancellors of God. In the Will work and acquire, and thou hast chained the wheel of Chance, and shall sit hereafter out of fear from her rotations. A political victory, a rise of rents, the recovery of your sick or the return of your absent friend, or some other favorable event raises your spirits, and you think good days are preparing for you. Do not believe it. Nothing can bring you peace but yourself. Nothing can bring you peace but the triumph of principles.

James Allen

~ ~

AS A MAN
THINKETH

FOREWORD

THIS little volume (the result of meditation and experience) is not intended as an exhaustive treatise on the much-written-upon subject of the power of thought. It is suggestive rather than explanatory, its object being to stimulate men and women to the discovery and perception of the truth that "They themselves are makers of themselves" by virtue of the thoughts which they choose and encourage; that mind is the master-weaver, both of the inner garment of character and the outer garment of circumstance, and that, as they may have hitherto woven in ignorance and pain they may now weave in enlightenment and happiness.

JAMES ALLEN

THOUGHT AND CHARACTER

THE APHORISM, "As a man thinketh in his heart so is he," not only embraces the whole of a man's being, but is so comprehensive as to reach out to every condition and circumstance of his life. A man is literally *what he thinks*, his character being the complete sum of all his thoughts.

As the plant springs from, and could not be without the seed, so every act of a man springs from the hidden seeds of thought, and could not have appeared without them. This applies equally to those acts called "spontaneous" and "unpremeditated" as to those which are deliberately executed.

Act is the blossom of thought, and joy and suffering are its fruits; thus does a man garner in the sweet and bitter fruitage of his own husbandry.

Thought in the mind hath made us. What we are
By thought was wrought and built. If a man's mind
Hath evil thoughts, pain comes on him as comes
The wheel the ox behind. . . . If one endure

*In purity of thought, joy follows him
As his own shadow—sure.*

Man is a growth by law, and not a creation by artifice, and cause and effect is as absolute and undeviating in the hidden realm of thought as in the world of visible and material things. A noble and Godlike character is not a thing of favor or chance, but is the natural result of continued effort in right thinking, the effect of long-cherished association with Godlike thoughts. An ignoble and bestial character, by the same process, is the result of the continued harboring of groveling thoughts.

Man is made or unmade by himself; in the armory of thought he forges the weapons by which he destroys himself; he also fashions the tools with which he builds for himself heavenly mansions of joy and strength and peace. By the right choice and true application of thought, man ascends to the Divine Perfection; by the abuse and wrong application of thought, he descends below the level of the beast. Between these two extremes are all the grades of character, and man is their maker and master.

Of all the beautiful truths pertaining to the soul which have been restored and brought to light in this age, none is more gladdening or fruitful of divine promise and confidence than this—that man is the master of thought, the molder of character, and the maker and shaper of condition, environment, and destiny.

As a being of Power, Intelligence, and Love, and the lord of his own thoughts, man holds the key to every situation, and contains within himself that transforming and regenerative agency by which he may make himself what he wills.

Man is always the master, even in his weakest and most abandoned state; but in his weakness and degradation he is the foolish master who misgoverns his household. When he begins to reflect upon his condition, and to search diligently for the Law upon which his being is established, he then becomes the wise master, directing his energies with intelligence, and fashioning his thought to fruitful issues. Such is the *conscious* master, and man can only thus become by discovering *within himself* the laws of thought; which discovery is totally a matter of application, self-analysis, and experience.

Only by much searching and mining are gold and diamonds obtained, and man can find every truth connected with his being if he will dig deep into the mine of his soul; and that he is the maker of his character, the molder of his life, and the builder of his destiny, he may unerringly prove, if he will watch, control, and alter his thoughts, tracing their effects upon himself, upon others, and upon his life and circumstances, linking cause and effect by patient practice and investigation, and utilizing his every experience, even to the most trivial, everyday occurrence, as a means of obtaining that knowledge of himself which is Understanding, Wisdom, Power. In this direction, as in no other, is the law absolute that "He that seeketh findeth; and to him that knocketh it shall be opened"; for only by patience, practice, and ceaseless importunity can a man enter the Door of the Temple of Knowledge.

EFFECT OF THOUGHT ON CIRCUMSTANCES

A MAN'S MIND may be likened to a garden, which may be intelligently cultivated or allowed to run wild; but whether cultivated or neglected, it must, and will, *bring forth*. If no useful seeds are *put* into it, then an abundance of useless weed-seeds will *fall* therein, and will continue to produce their kind.

Just as a gardener cultivates his plot, keeping it free from weeds, and growing the flowers and fruits which he requires, so may a man tend the garden of his mind, weeding out all the wrong, useless, and impure thoughts, and cultivating toward perfection the flowers and fruits of right, useful, and pure thoughts. By pursuing this process, a man sooner or later discovers that he is the master-gardener of his soul, the director of his life. He also reveals, within himself, the laws of thought, and understands, with ever-increasing accuracy, how the thought-forces and mind-elements operate in the shaping of his character, circumstances, and destiny.

Thought and character are one, and as character can only manifest and discover itself through environment and circumstance, the outer conditions of a person's life will always be found to be harmoniously related to his inner state. This does not mean that a man's circumstances at any given time are an indication of his *entire* character, but that those circumstances are so intimately connected with some vital thought-element within himself that, for the time being, they are indispensable to his development.

Every man is where he is by the law of his being; the thoughts which he has built into his character have brought him there, and in the arrangement of his life there is no element of chance, but all is the result of a law which cannot err. Tis is just as true of those who feel "out of harmony" with their surroundings as of those who are contented with them.

As a progressive and evolving being, man is where he is that he may learn that he may grow; and as he learns the spiritual lesson which any circumstance contains for him, it passes away and gives place to other circumstances.

Man is buffeted by circumstances so long as he believes himself to be the creature of outside conditions, but when he realizes that he is a creative power, and that he may command the hidden soil and seeds of his being out of which circumstances grow, he then becomes the rightful master of himself.

That circumstances grow out of thought every man knows who has for any length of time practiced self-control and self-purification, for he will have noticed that the alteration in his circumstances has been in exact ratio with his altered mental condition. So true is this that when a man earnestly applies himself to remedy the defects in his character, and makes swift and marked progress, he passes rapidly through a succession of vicissitudes.

The soul attracts that which it secretly harbors; that which it loves, and also that which it fears; it reaches the height of its cherished aspirations; it falls to the level of its unchastened desires, and circumstances are the means by which the soul receives its own.

Every thought-seed sown or allowed to fall into the mind, and to take root there, produces its own, blossoming sooner or later into act, and bearing its own fruitage of opportunity and circumstance. Good thoughts bear good fruit, bad thoughts bad fruit.

The outer world of circumstance shapes itself to the inner world of thought, and both pleasant and unpleasant external conditions are factors which make for the ultimate good of the individual. As the reaper of his own harvest, man learns both by suffering and bliss.

Following the inmost desires, aspirations, thoughts, by which he allows himself to be dominated (pursuing the will-o'-the-wisps of impure imagining or steadfastly walking the highway of strong and high endeavor), a man at last arrives at their fruition and fulfillment in the outer condition of his life.

The laws of growth and adjustment everywhere obtain.

A man does not come to the almshouse or the jail by the tyranny of fate or circumstance, but by the pathway of groveling thoughts and base desires. Nor does a pure-minded man fall suddenly into crime by stress of any mere external force; the criminal thought had long been secretly fostered in the heart, and the hour of opportunity revealed its gathered power. Circumstance does not make the man; it reveals him to himself. No such conditions can exist as descending into vice and its attendant sufferings apart from vicious inclinations; or ascending into virtue and its pure happiness without the continued cultivation of virtuous aspirations; and man, therefore, as the lord and master of thought, is the maker of himself, the shaper and author of environment. Even at birth the soul comes to its own, and through every step of its earthly pilgrimage it attracts those combinations of conditions which reveal itself, which are the reflections of its own purity and impurity, its strength and weakness.

Men do not attract that which they *want*, but that which they *are*. Their whims, fancies, and ambitions are thwarted at every step, but their inmost thoughts and desires are fed with their own food, be it foul or clean. The "divinity that shapes our ends" is in ourselves; it is our very self. Man is manacled only by himself: thought and action are the jailers of Fate—they imprison, being base; they are also the angels of Freedom—they liberate, being noble.

Not what he wishes and prays for does a man get, but what he justly earns. His wishes and prayers are only gratified and answered when they harmonize with his thoughts and actions.

In the light of this truth, what, then, is the meaning of "fighting against circumstances"? It means that a man is continually revolting against an *effect* without, while all the time he is nourishing and preserving its *cause* in his heart.

That cause may take the form of a conscious vice or an unconscious weakness; but whatever it is, it stubbornly retards the efforts of its possessor, and thus calls aloud for remedy.

Men are anxious to improve their circumstances, but are unwilling to improve themselves; they therefore remain bound. The man who does not shrink from self-crucifixion can never fail to accomplish the object upon which his heart is set. This is as true of earthly as of heavenly things. Even the man whose sole object is to acquire wealth must be prepared to make great personal sacrifices before he can accomplish his object; and how much more so he who would realize a strong and well-poised life?

Here is a man who is wretchedly poor. He is extremely anxious that his surroundings and home comforts should be improved, yet all the time he shirks his work, and considers he is justified in trying to deceive his employer on the ground of the insufficiency of his wages. Such a man does not understand the simplest rudiments of those principles which are the basis of true prosperity, and is not only totally unfitted to rise out of his wretchedness, but is actually attracting to himself a still deeper wretchedness by dwelling in, and acting out, indolent, deceptive, and unmanly thoughts.

Here is a rich man who is the victim of a painful and persistent disease as the result of gluttony. He is willing to give large sums of money to get rid of it, but he will not sacrifice his gluttonous desires. He wants to gratify his taste for rich and unnatural viands and have his health as well. Such a man is totally unfit to have health, because he has not yet learned the first principles of a healthy life.

Here is an employer of labor who adopts crooked measures to avoid paying the regulation wage, and, in the hope of making larger profits, reduces the wages of his work-people. Such a man is altogether unfitted for prosperity, and when he finds himself bankrupt, both as regards reputation and riches, he blames circumstances, not knowing that he is the sole author of his condition.

I have introduced these three cases merely as illustrative of the truth that man is the causer (though nearly always unconsciously) of his circumstances, and that, whilst aiming at a good end, he is continually frustrating its accomplishment by encouraging thoughts and desires which cannot possibly harmonize with that end. Such cases could be multiplied and varied almost indefinitely, but this is not necessary, as the reader can, if he so resolves, trace the action of the laws of thought in his own mind and life, and until this is done, mere external facts cannot serve as a ground of reasoning.

Circumstances, however, are so complicated, thought is so deeply rooted, and the conditions of happiness vary so vastly with individuals, that a man's *entire* soul-condition (although it may be known to himself) cannot be judged by another from the external aspect of his life alone. A man may be honest in certain directions, yet suffer privations; a man may be dishonest in certain directions, yet acquire wealth; but the conclusion usually formed that the one man fails *because of his particular honesty,* and that the other prospers *because of his particular dishonesty,* is the result of a superficial judgment, which assumes that the dishonest man is almost totally corrupt, and the honest man almost entirely virtuous. In the light of a deeper knowledge and wider experience, such judgment is found to be erroneous. The dishonest man may have some admirable virtues which the other does not possess; and the honest man obnoxious vices which are absent in the other. The honest man reaps the good results of his honest thoughts and acts; he also brings upon himself the sufferings which his vices produce. The dishonest man likewise garners his own suffering and happiness.

It is pleasing to human vanity to believe that one suffers because of one's virtue; but not until a man has extirpated every sickly, bitter, and impure thought from his mind, and washed every sinful stain from his soul, can he be in a position to know and declare that his sufferings are the result of his good, and not of his bad qualities; and on the way to, yet long before he has reached, that supreme perfection, he will have found, working in his mind and life, the Great Law which is absolutely just, and which cannot, therefore, give good for evil, evil for good. Possessed of such knowledge, he will then know, looking back upon his past ignorance and blindness, that his life is, and always was, justly ordered, and that all his past experiences, good and bad, were the equitable outworking of his evolving, yet unevolved self.

Good thoughts and actions can never produce bad results; bad thoughts and actions can never produce good results. This is but saying that nothing can come from corn but corn, nothing from nettles but nettles. Men understand this law in the natural world, and work with it; but few understand it in the mental and moral world (thought its operation there is just as simple and undeviating), and they, therefore, do not cooperate with it.

Suffering is *always* the effect of wrong thought in some direction. It is an indication that the individual is out of harmony with himself, with the Law of his being. The sole and supreme use of suffering is to purify, to burn out all that is useless and impure. Suffering ceases for him who is pure. There could be no object in burning gold after the dross had been removed, and a perfectly pure and enlightened being could not suffer.

The circumstances which a man encounters with suffering are the result of his own mental inharmony. The circumstances which a man encounters with blessedness are the result of his own mental harmony. Blessedness, not material possessions, is the measure of right thought; wretchedness, not lack of material possessions, is the measure of wrong thought. A man may be cursed and rich; he may be blessed and poor. Blessedness and riches are only joined together when the riches are rightly and wisely used; and the poor man only descends into wretchedness when he regards his lot as a burden unjustly imposed.

Indigence and indulgence are the two extremes of wretchedness. They are both equally unnatural and the result of mental disorder. A man is not rightly conditioned until he is a happy, healthy, and prosperous being; and happiness, health, and prosperity are the result of a harmonious adjustment of the inner with the outer, of the man with his surroundings.

A man only begins to be a man when he ceases to whine and revile, and commences to search for the hidden justice which regulates his life.

And as he adapts his mind to that regulating factor, he ceases to accuse others as the cause of his condition, and builds himself up in strong and noble thoughts; ceases to kick against circumstances, but begins to use them as aids to his more rapid progress, and as a means of discovering the hidden powers and possibilities within himself.

Law, not confusion, is the dominating principle in the universe; justice, not injustice, is the soul and substance of life; and righteousness, not corruption, is the molding and moving force in the spiritual government of the world. This being so, man has but to right himself to find that the universe is right; and during the process of putting himself right, he will find that as he alters his thoughts toward things and other people, things and other people will alter towards him.

The proof of this truth is in every person, and it therefore admits of easy investigation by systematic introspection and self-analysis. Let a man radically alter his thoughts, and he will be astonished at the rapid transformation it will effect in the material conditions of his life. Men imagine that thought can be kept secret, but it cannot; it rapidly crystallizes into habit, and habit solidifies into circumstance. Bestial thoughts crystallize into habits of drunkenness and sensuality, which solidify into circumstances of destitution and disease: impure thoughts of every kind crystallize into enervating and confusing habits, which solidify into distracting and adverse circumstances: thoughts of fear, doubt, and indecision crystallize into weak, unmanly, and irresolute habits which solidify into circumstances of failure, indigence, and slavish dependence: lazy thoughts crystallize into habits of uncleanliness and dishonesty, which solidify into circumstances of foulness and beggary: hateful and condemnatory thoughts crystallize into habits of accusations and violence, which solidify into circumstances of injury and persecution: selfish thoughts of all kinds crystallize into habits of self-seeking which solidify into circumstances more or less distressing. On the other hand, beautiful thoughts of all kinds crystallize into habits of grace and kindliness, which solidify into genial and sunny circumstances: pure thoughts crystallize into habits of temperance and self-control, which solidify into circumstances of repose and peace: thoughts of courage, self-reliance, and decision crystallize into manly habits, which solidify into circumstances of success, plenty, and freedom: energetic thoughts crystallize into habits of cleanliness and industry, which solidify into circumstances of pleasantness: gentle and forgiving thoughts crystallize into habits of gentleness, which solidify into protective and preservative circumstances: loving and unselfish thoughts crystallize into habits of self-forgetfulness for others, which solidify into circumstances of sure and abiding prosperity and true riches.

A particular train of thought persisted in, be it good or bad, cannot fail to produce its results on the character and circumstances. A man cannot *directly* choose his circumstances, but he can choose his thoughts, and so indirectly, yet surely, shape his circumstances.

Nature helps every man to the gratification of the thoughts which he most encourages, and opportunities are presented which will most speedily bring to the surface both the good and evil thoughts.

Let a man cease from his sinful thoughts, and all the world will soften towards him, and be ready to help him; let him put away his weakly and sickly thoughts, and lo! opportunities will spring up on every hand to aid his strong resolves; let him encourage good thoughts, and no hard fate shall bind him down to wretchedness and shame. The world is your kaleidoscope, and the varying combinations of colors which at every succeeding moment it presents to you are the exquisitely adjusted pictures of your ever-moving thoughts.

> You will be what you will to be;
>   Let failure find its false content
>   In that poor word, "environment,"
> But spirit scorns it, and is free.
>
> It masters time, it conquers space;
>   It cows that boastful trickster, Chance,
>   And bids the tyrant Circumstance
> Uncrown, and fill a servant's place.
>
> The human Will, that force unseen,
>   The offspring of a deathless Soul,
>   Can hew a way to any goal,
> Though walls of granite intervene.

Be not impatient in delay,
  But wait as one who understands;
  When spirit rises and commands,
The gods are ready to obey.

EFFECT OF THOUGHT ON HEALTH AND THE BODY

THE BODY is the servant of the mind. It obeys the operations of the mind, whether they be deliberately chosen or automatically expressed. At the bidding of unlawful thoughts the body sinks rapidly into disease and decay; at the command of glad and beautiful thoughts it becomes clothed with youthfulness and beauty.

Disease and health, like circumstances, are rooted in thought. Sickly thoughts will express themselves through a sickly body. Thoughts of fear have been known to kill a man as speedily as a bullet, and they are continually killing thousands of people just as surely though less rapidly. The people who live in fear of disease are the people who get it. Anxiety quickly demoralizes the whole body, and lays it open to the creature of disease; while impure thoughts, even if not physically indulged, will soon shatter the nervous system.

Strong, pure, and happy thoughts build up the body in vigor and grace. The body is a delicate and plastic instrument, which responds readily to the thoughts by which it is impressed, and habits of thought will produce their own effects, good or bad, upon it.

Men will continue to have impure and poisoned blood so long as they propagate unclean thoughts. Out of a clean heart comes a clean life and a clean body. Out of a defiled mind proceeds a defiled life and a corrupt body. Thought is the fount of action, life and manifestations; make the fountain pure, and all will be pure.

Change of diet will not help a man who will not change his thoughts. When a man makes his thoughts pure, he no longer desires impure food.

Clean thoughts make clean habits. The so-called saint who does not wash his body is not a saint. He who has strengthened and purified his thoughts does not need to consider the malevolent microbe.

If you would perfect your body, guard your mind. If you would renew your body, beautify your mind. Thoughts of malice, envy, disappointment, despondency, rob the body of its health and grace. A sour face does not come by chance; it is made by sour thoughts.

Wrinkles that mar are drawn by folly, passion, pride.

I know a woman of ninety-six who has the

bright, innocent face of a girl. I know a man well under middle age whose face is drawn into inharmonious contours. The one is the result of a sweet and sunny disposition; the other is the outcome of passion and discontent.

As you cannot have a sweet and wholesome abode unless you admit the air and sunshine freely into your rooms, so a strong body and a bright, happy, or serene countenance can only result from the free admittance into the mind of thoughts of joy and good will and serenity.

On the faces of the aged there are wrinkles made by sympathy; others by strong and pure thought; and other are carved by passion: who cannot distinguish them? With those who have lived righteously, age is calm, peaceful, and softly mellowed, like the setting sun. I have recently seen a philosopher on his deathbed. He was not old except in years. He died as sweetly and peacefully as he had lived.

There is no physician like cheerful thought for dissipating the ills of the body; there is no comforter to compare with good will for dispersing the shadows of grief and sorrow. To live continually in thoughts of ill will, cynicism, suspicion, and envy, is to be confined in a self-made prisonhole. But to think well of all, to be cheerful with all, to patiently learn to find the good in all—such unselfish thoughts are the very portals of heaven; and to dwell day by day in thoughts of peace toward every creature will bring abounding peace to their possessor.

THOUGHT AND PURPOSE

UNTIL THOUGHT is linked with purpose there is no intelligent accomplishment. With the majority the barque of thought is allowed to drift upon the ocean of life. Aimlessness is a vice, and such drifting must not continue for him who would steer clear of catastrophe and destruction.

They who have no central purpose in their life fall an easy prey to petty worries, fears, troubles, and self-pitying, all of which lead, just as surely as deliberately planned sins (though by a different route), to failure, unhappiness, and loss, for weakness cannot persist in a power-evolving universe.

A man should conceive of a legitimate purpose in his heart, and set out to accomplish it. He should make this purpose the centralizing point of his thoughts. It may take the form of a spiritual ideal, or it may be a worldly object, according to his nature at the time being; but whichever it is, he should steadily focus his thought-forces upon the object which he has set before him. He should make this purpose his supreme duty, and should devote himself to its attainment, not allowing his thoughts to wander away into ephemeral fancies, longings, and imaginings. This is the royal road to self-control and true concentration of thought. Even if he fails again and again to accomplish his purpose (as he necessarily must until weakness is overcome), the *strength of character gained* will be the measure of his *true* success, and this will form a new starting-point for future power and triumph.

Those who are not prepared for the apprehension of a *great* purpose should fix their thoughts upon the faultless performance of their duty, no matter how insignificant their task may appear. Only in this way can the thoughts be gathered and focused, and resolution and energy be developed, which being done, there is nothing which may not be accomplished.

The weakest soul, knowing its own weakness, and believing this truth—*that strength can only be developed by effort and practice,* will, thus believing, at once begin to exert itself, and, adding effort to effort, patience to patience, and strength to strength, will never cease to develop, and will at last grow divinely strong.

As the physically weak man can make himself strong by careful and patient training, so the man of weak thoughts can make them strong by exercising himself in right thinking.

To put away aimlessness and weakness, and to begin to think with purpose, is to enter the ranks of those strong ones who only recognize failure as one of the pathways to attainment; who make all conditions serve them, and who think strongly, attempt fearlessly, and accomplish masterfully.

Having conceived of his purpose, a man should mentally mark out a *straight* pathway to its achievement, looking neither to the right nor the left. Doubts and fears should be rigorously excluded; they are disintegrating elements which break up the straight line of effort, rendering it crooked, ineffectual, useless. Thoughts of doubt and fear never accomplish anything, and never can. They always lead to failure. Purpose, energy, power to do, and all strong thoughts cease when doubt and fear creep in.

The will to do springs from the knowledge that we *can* do. Doubt and fear are the great enemies of knowledge, and he who encourages them, who does not slay them, thwarts himself at every step.

He who has conquered doubt and fear has conquered failure. His every thought is allied with power, and all difficulties are bravely met and wisely overcome. His purposes are seasonably planted, and they bloom and bring forth fruit which does not fall prematurely to the ground.

Thought allied fearlessly to purpose becomes creative force: he who *knows* this is ready to become something higher and stronger than a mere bundle of wavering thoughts and fluctuating sensations; he who *does* this has become the conscious and intelligent wielder of his mental powers.

THE THOUGHT-FACTOR IN ACHIEVEMENT

ALL THAT a man achieves and all that he fails to achieve is the direct result of his own thoughts. In a justly ordered universe, where loss of equipoise would mean total destruction, individual responsibility must be absolute. A man's weakness and strength, purity and impurity, are his own, and not another man's; they are brought about by himself, and not by another; and they can only be altered by himself, never by another. His condition is also his own, and not another man's. His suffering and his happiness are evolved from within. As he thinks, so he is; as he continues to think, so he remains.

A strong man cannot help a weaker unless that weaker is *willing* to be helped, and even then the weak man must become strong of himself; he must, by his own efforts, develop the strength which he admires in another. None but himself can alter his condition.

It has been usual for men to think and to say, "Many men are slaves because one is an oppressor; let us hate the oppressor." Now, however, there is amongst an increasing few a tendency to reverse this judgment, and to say, "One man is an oppressor because many are slaves; let us despise the slaves." The truth is that oppressor and slave are co-operators in ignorance, and, while seeming to afflict each other, are in reality afflicting themselves. A perfect Knowledge perceives the action of law in the weakness of the oppressed and the misapplied power of the oppressor; a perfect Love, seeing the suffering which both states entail, condemns neither; a perfect Compassion embraces both oppressor and oppressed.

He who has conquered weakness, and has put away all selfish thoughts, belongs neither to oppressor nor oppressed. He is free.

A man can only rise, conquer, and achieve by lifting up his thoughts. He can only remain weak, and abject, and miserable, by refusing to lift up his thoughts.

Before a man can achieve anything, even in worldly things, he must lift his thoughts above slavish animal indulgence. He may not, in order to succeed, give up *all* animality and selfishness, by any means; but a portion of it must, at least, be sacrificed. A man whose first thought is bestial indulgence could neither think clearly nor plan methodically; he could not find and develop his latent resources, and would fail in any undertaking. Not having commenced manfully to control his thoughts, he is not in a position to control affairs and to adopt serious responsibilities. He is not fit to act independently and stand alone. But he is limited only by the thoughts which he chooses.

There can be no progress, no achievement without sacrifice, and a man's worldly success will be in the measure that he sacrifices his confused animal thoughts, and fixes his mind on the development of his plans, and the strengthening of his resolution and self-reliance. And the higher he lifts his thoughts, the more manly, upright, and righteous he becomes, the greater will be his success, the more blessed and enduring will be his achievements.

The universe does not favor the greedy, the dishonest, the vicious, although on the mere surface it may sometimes appear to do so; it helps the honest, the magnanimous, the virtuous. All the great teachers of the ages have declared this in varying forms, and to prove and know it a man has but to persist in making himself more and more virtuous by lifting up his thoughts.

Intellectual achievements are the result of thought consecrated to the search for knowledge, or for the beautiful and true in life and nature. Such achievements may be sometimes connected with vanity and ambition, but they are not the outcome of those characteristics; they are the natural outgrowth of long and arduous effort, and of pure and unselfish thoughts.

Spiritual achievements are the consummation of holy aspirations. He who lives constantly in the conception of noble and lofty thoughts, who dwells upon all that is pure and unselfish, will, as surely as the sun reaches its zenith and the moon its full, become wise and noble in character, and rise into a position of influence and blessedness.

Achievement, of whatever kind, is the crown of effort, the diadem of thought. By the aid of self-control, resolution, purity, righteousness, and well-directed thought a man ascends; by the aid of animality, indolence, impurity, corruption, and confusion of thought a man descends.

A man may rise to high success in the world, and even to lofty altitudes in the spiritual realm, and again descend into weakness and wretchedness by allowing arrogant, selfish, and corrupt thoughts to take possession of him.

Victories attained by right thought can only be maintained by watchfulness. Many give way when success is assured, and rapidly fall back into failure.

All achievements, whether in the business, intellectual, or spiritual world, are the result of definitely directed thought, are governed by the same law and are of the same method; the only difference lies in *the object of attainment*. He who would accomplish little must sacrifice little; he who would achieve much must sacrifice much, he who would attain highly must sacrifice greatly.

VISIONS AND IDEALS

THE DREAMERS are the saviors of the world. As the visible world is sustained by the invisible, so men, through all their trials and sins and sordid vocations, are nourished by the beautiful visions of their solitary dreamers. Humanity cannot forget its dreamers; it cannot let their ideals fade and die; it lives in them; it knows them as the *realities* which it shall one day see and know.

Composer, sculptor, painter, poet, prophet, sage, these are the makers of the after-world, the architects of heaven. The world is beautiful because they have lived; without them, laboring humanity would perish.

He who cherishes a beautiful vision, a lofty ideal in his heart, will one day realize it. Columbus cherished a vision of another world, and he discovered it; Copernicus fostered the vision of a multiplicity of worlds and a wider universe and he revealed it; Buddha beheld the vision of a spiritual world of stainless beauty and perfect peace, and he entered into it.

Cherish your visions; cherish your ideals; cherish the music that stirs in your heart, the beauty that forms in your mind, the loveliness that drapes your purest thoughts, for out of them will grow all delightful conditions, all heavenly environment; of these, if you but remain true to them, your world will at last be built.

To desire is to obtain; to aspire is to achieve. Shall man's basest desires receive the fullest measure of gratification, and his purest aspirations starve for lack of sustenance? Such is not the law: such a condition of things can never obtain: "Ask and receive."

Dream lofty dreams, and as you dream, so shall you become. Your Vision is the promise of what you shall one day be; your Ideal is the prophecy of what you shall at last unveil.

The greatest achievement was at first and for a time a dream. The oak sleeps in the acorn; the bird waits in the egg; and in the highest vision of the soul a waking angel stirs. Dreams are the seedlings of realities.

Your circumstances may be uncongenial, but they shall not long remain so if you but perceive an Ideal and strive to reach it. You cannot travel *within* and stand still *without*. Here is a youth hard pressed by poverty and labor; confined long hours in an unhealthy workshop; un-schooled, and lacking all the arts of refinement. But he dreams of better things; he thinks of intelligence, of refinement, of grace and beauty. He conceives of, mentally builds up, an ideal condition of life; the vision of a wider liberty and a larger scope takes possession of him; unrest urges him to action, and he utilizes all his spare time and means, small though they are, to the development of his latent powers and resources. Very soon so altered has his mind become that the workshop can no longer hold him. It has become so out of harmony with his mentality that it falls out of his life as a garment is cast aside, and, with the growth of opportunities which fit the scope of his expanding powers, he passes out of it forever. Years later we see this youth as a full-grown man. We find him a master of certain forces of the mind which he wields with world-wide influence and almost unequaled power. In his hands he holds the cords of gigantic responsibilities; he speaks, and lo! lives are changed; men and women hang upon his words and remold their characters, and, sunlike, he becomes the fixed and luminous center round which innumerable destinies revolve.

He has realized the Vision of his youth. He has become one with his Ideal.

And you, too, youthful reader, will realize the Vision (not the idle wish) of your heart, be it base or beautiful, or a mixture of both, for you will always gravitate toward that which you, secretly, most love. Into your hands will be placed the exact results of your own thoughts; you will receive that which you earn; no more, no less. Whatever your present environment may be, you will fall, remain, or rise with your thoughts, your Vision, your Ideal. You will become as small as your controlling desire; as great as your dominant aspiration: in the beautiful words of Stanton Kirkham Davis, "You may be keeping accounts, and presently you shall walk out of the door that for so long has seemed to you the barrier of your ideals, and shall find yourself before an audience—the pen still behind your ear, the inkstains on your fingers—and then and there shall pour out the torrent of your inspiration. You may be driving sheep, and you shall wander to the city—bucolic and open-mouthed; shall wander under the intrepid guidance of the spirit into the studio of the master, and after a time he shall say, 'I have nothing more to teach you.' And now you have become the master, who did so recently dream of great things while driving sheep. You shall lay down the saw and the plane to take upon yourself the regeneration of the world."

The thoughtless, the ignorant, and the indolent, seeing only the apparent effects of things and not the things themselves, talk of luck, of fortune, and chance. Seeing a man grow rich, they say, "How lucky he is!" Observing another become intellectual, they exclaim, "How highly favored he is!" And noting the saintly character and wide influence of another, they remark, "How chance aids him at every turn!" They do not see the trials and failures and struggles which these men have voluntarily encountered in order to gain their experience; have no knowledge of the sacrifices they have made, of the undaunted efforts they have put forth, of the faith they have exercised, that they might overcome the apparently insurmountable, and realize the Vision of their heart. They do not know the darkness and the heartaches; they only see the light and joy, and call it "luck"; do not see the long and arduous journey, but only behold the pleasant goal, and call it "good fortune"; do not understand the process, but only perceive the result, and call it "chance."

In all human affairs there are *efforts,* and there are *results,* and the strength of the effort is the measure of the result. Chance is not. "Gifts," powers, material, intellectual, and spiritual possessions are the fruits of effort; they are thoughts completed, objects accomplished, visions realized.

The Vision that you glorify in your mind, the Ideal that you enthrone in your heart—this you will build your life by, this you will become.

SERENITY

CALMNESS OF mind is one of the beautiful jewels of wisdom. It is the result of long and patient effort in self-control. Its presence is an indication of ripened experience, and of a more than ordinary knowledge of the laws and operations of thought.

A man becomes calm in the measure that he understands himself as a thought-evolved being, for such knowledge necessitates the understanding of others as the result of thought, and as he develops a right understanding, and sees more and more clearly the internal relations of things by the action of cause and effect, he ceases to fuss and fume and worry and grieve, and remains-poised, steadfast, serene.

The calm man, having learned how to govern himself, knows how to adapt himself to others; and they, in turn, reverence his spiritual strength, and feel that they can learn of him and rely upon him. The more tranquil a man becomes, the greater is his success, his influence, his power for good. Even the ordinary trader will find his business prosperity increase as he develops a greater self-control and equanimity, for people will always prefer to deal with a man whose demeanor is strongly equable.

The strong, calm man is always loved and revered. He is like a shade-giving tree in a thirsty land, or a sheltering rock in a storm. "Who does not love a tranquil heart, a sweet-tempered, balanced life? It does not matter whether it rains or shines, or what changes come to those possessing these blessings, for they are always sweet, serene, and calm. That exquisite poise of character which we call serenity is the last lesson of culture; it is the flowering of life, the fruitage of the soul. It is precious as wisdom, more to be desired than gold—yea, than even fine gold. How insignificant mere money-seeking looks in comparison with a serene life—a life that dwells in the ocean of Truth, beneath the waves, beyond the reach of tempests, in the Eternal Calm!

"How many people we know who sour their lives, who ruin all that is sweet and beautiful by explosive tempers, who destroy their poise of character, and make bad blood! It is a question whether the great majority of people do not ruin their lives and mar their happiness by lack of self-control. How few people we meet in life who are well-balanced, who have that exquisite poise which is characteristic of the finished character!"

Yes, humanity surges with uncontrolled passion, is tumultuous with ungoverned grief, is blown about by anxiety and doubt. Only the wise man, only he whose thoughts are controlled and purified, makes the winds and the storms of the soul obey him.

Tempest-tossed souls, wherever ye may be, under whatsoever conditions ye may live, know this—in the ocean of life the isles of Blessedness are smiling, and the sunny shore of your ideal awaits your coming. Keep your hand firmly upon the helm of thought. In the barque of your soul reclines the commanding Master; He does but sleep; wake Him. Self-control is strength; Right Thought is mastery; Calmness is power. Say unto your heart, "Peace, be still!"

THE PIVOT FAMILY CLASSICS SERIES

INEXPENSIVE EDITIONS . . .
COMPLETE AND UNABRIDGED

☐ **ABIDE IN CHRIST** by Andrew Murray. The famous book in which the author writes about the true meaning of the words "abide in me." Introduction by William J. Petersen, editor of *Eternity* magazine. **95¢**

☐ **DAILY STRENGTH FOR DAILY NEEDS** by Mary W. Tileston. Each page, one for every day of the year, strikes a note of comfort and assurance for today, and hope and confidence for tomorrow. Treasured by countless readers for nearly a century, an endless source of insight and inspiration. **$1.25**

☐ **GOLD DUST** by Charlotte Yonge. Daily reminders of Divine love, brief but memorable restatements of the truths the heart knows but the mind may forget. A storehouse of faith and understanding for the whole family. **95¢**

☐ **IN HIS STEPS** by Charles M. Sheldon. A new edition of the most popular novel ever written, with an inspiring introduction by Donald T. Kauffman. **95¢**

☐ **IN TUNE WITH THE INFINITE** by Ralph Waldo Trine. Drawing on his inspired understanding of Scripture, the author points out the way to peace of mind, in one of the inspirational classics of all time. **$1.25**

☐ **KEPT FOR THE MASTER'S USE** by Frances Ridley Havergal. Twelve paths to participating in God's mighty promise, in a book of lasting inspiration and guidance. **95¢**

☐ **OF THE IMITATION OF CHRIST** by Thomas à Kempis. The most famous book of devotions in Christendom. Meditations on the life and teachings of Jesus and second only to the Bible as a guide and inspiration. **95¢**

☐ **THE PILGRIM'S PROGRESS** by John Bunyan. An exciting larger-than-life adventure story and a document of faith and inspiration. Introduction by Donald T. Kauffman. **95¢**

☐ **WHAT ALL THE WORLD'S A-SEEKING** by Ralph Waldo Trine. The one great principle of life and how it can be understood and used. A truly "how to" for those who will open themselves to the chance for joy and peace. **$1.25**

Buy them at your bookstore or use this handy coupon